IDEAS
General Editor: Jonathan Rée

Social Philosophy

# Social Philosophy

HANS FINK

METHUEN
LONDON AND NEW YORK

First published in 1981 by
Methuen & Co. Ltd
11 New Fetter Lane,
London EC4P 4EE

Published in the USA by
Methuen & Co.
in association with Methuen, Inc.
733 Third Avenue, New York,
NY10017

© 1981 Hans Fink

Printed in Great Britain by
Richard Clay
(The Chaucer Press), Ltd,
Bungay, Suffolk

*British Library Cataloguing in
Publication Data*
Fink, Hans
Social philosophy.
1. Social sciences
1. Title
300'.1 HG1
ISBN 0-416-71990-2
ISBN 0-416 71000-5 Pbk

# Contents

# Acknowledgements

The raw manuscript of this book was written in my best English on the basis of – though by no means as a translation of – a somewhat similar book which I published in Danish in 1975. Jonathan Rée went through the manuscript with me, line by line and word by word, and made innumerable corrections and suggestions. I am extremely grateful to him for this and for much else besides. I should also like to thank Asta Fink, Lena Frikke, Jean McCrindle, Johs Østergaard Petersen, Kirsten Rajczyk and Helmuth Schledermann for their help at various stages in the writing of this book.

16 November 1980 H.F.

# 1
# Introduction

All of us have experienced quite dramatic social changes in our lifetimes. Our families differ greatly from those of our parents, however anxious we may be to preserve traditional values. Most of those who live on their own or in groups other than families do so in ways which were impossible a generation ago. People who have been working for more than a few years have almost certainly experienced changes in their actual work and working conditions. The unemployed are in a quite different position from that of the unemployed of former decades – as they are often reminded. The natural environment has been rearranged and interfered with more thoroughly in the third quarter of this century than ever before. In many countries the political framework has changed fundamentally within living memory, and everywhere the laws we are supposed to obey change more rapidly than ever before, and not only in points of detail. Manhood suffrage without property qualifications was the exception rather than the rule one hundred years ago, and it was our mothers or grandmothers who demanded and got the vote for women. All these changes are part of an immensely complex social process, the origins of which can be traced as far back in prehistory as human knowledge goes, and the process is likely to continue as long again, unless it is abruptly ended by an attempt to defend humanity with nuclear arms.

The social process is the life of human beings, their birth, procreation and death, and their production and distribution which must continue as long as human life continues. Changes in the social process are changes in the conditions of life, in the organization of reproduction, production and distribution and in the ways people experience and conceptualize their lives. We have all lived through changes of this kind and if we look at broader spans of the social process the differences become much greater. A delivery by a caesarean section in a New York clinic is worlds apart from a birth on Manhattan Island in the fifteenth century. Digging worms with a stick for personal consumption is one thing and feeding a computer eight hours a day in order to pay the rent is another. But amidst all these changes people continue to be born, have children, work, exchange goods and services and eventually die irrespective of how they have lived and of the categories in which they have thought about their lives, if, indeed, they have thought about them at all.

Our lives are a continuation of the lives of our forefathers and foremothers; but the material conditions and the social organization of our lives and our ideas about life in society are different from theirs. They are not completely different, though, both because their activity produced material and social structures some of which are still with us, and because their thinking produced ideas and conceptions which form the starting point for our own thinking. Our own activities and thinking are thus heavily dependent upon the past. This past provides the basis on which we can try to make things happen, or react to things happening, in the hope of making things better than they would otherwise be.

There are many different ways in which people may come to feel the need for social change. It may be a vague feeling of personal frustration, or a firm commitment to some theoretical analysis. But if we are to do something effective about it, two things are important. First, we need to know how and why things have come to be the way they are. Second, we should try to ensure that our feelings and commitments are shared by other people, perhaps only a few, but possibly by many thousands if the change which interests us is of wide social significance.

Some ideas of social change suggest a radical break with existing forms of social organization, demanding either a completely new arrangement or a return to 'the good old days before the rot set in'. Others defend the existing order as the best of all possible systems, or at least the least evil, but suggest minor adjustments to ensure its smooth running. But all of them claim to articulate the long-term interests of society as a whole even if some of them obviously express the interests of quite small social groups.

The programmes of political parties and social movements are attempts to formulate consistent platforms or guidelines for joint action. Usually they offer both an attempt at an analysis of the way things are going, and suggestions about desirable ends and means for the future. Social philosophy is about the fundamental issues on which political programmes divide: it is about what the principles of social life ought to be and why. When discussions between, say, liberals and socialists, or between communists and the new left, or between socialists and feminists, are pushed beyond surface polemics, or debates about tactics, they become discussions of social philosophy.

Questions of social philosophy can be asked quite abstractly: how are the relations between men and women, parents and children to be conceived of? What principles ought to govern the social distribution of labour, land, tools and products? What are the laws, and under what conditions are they valid? What, if anything, makes governments necessary? Put in this abstract manner, such questions can be said to have been under discussion since the very first human reflections on life in society. But the point of asking them varies enormously from one period to another. For instance, the question of how the relation between men and women should be understood can be raised today in ways which have never been possible before, and large-scale automation of the labour-process gives a new dimension to questions about the distribution of labour. It is possible to consider such questions in the abstract, but the social implications of any abstract answer will differ from one society to another. For instance, abstract arguments in favour of land being exclusively private property would mean different things in fifteenth- and nineteenth-century England, and in England, the USA, the USSR, Poland, India, China, North Vietnam, South Vietnam, Kampuchea, Iran or Zimbabwe today.

Social philosophy therefore needs to be historically informed. It is impossible to understand the social philosophies of today – including your own social philosophy – without knowledge of their roots both in the organization of present societies and in the social philosophies of the past. It is impossible to understand the organization of your own society without knowing something about the past which has produced the present; and it is impossible to understand a social philosophy without knowing the society within which it was elaborated and the actual problems to which it was addressed.

This introduction to social philosophy gives an account of several highly influential systems of social philosophy which serve as landmarks for the orientation of modern discussions. My descriptions of various stages in the history of social philosophy are set within an account of the changing social environment. The account is limited to the European tradition of social philosophy from the

Middle Ages to the present. One could say that it describes the rise and fall of the free market as the central social institution and as the key to the understanding of society.

By referring to the general tradition of social philosophy rather than the more specialized traditions of moral philosophy, political philosophy, or the philosophy of law, of history or of the social sciences, I wish to emphasize the fundamental unity of these different kinds of reflections on society. And in presenting philosophy as an integral part of the social process I hope to avoid the mistake of regarding philosophy either as so exalted that it is above political struggle or as so abstruse that it is irrelevant to it.

# 2

# Feudalism and the social philosophy of Aquinas

## Western Europe 800-1000: the rise of the fief

During the ninth century Western Europe was hit by a series of invasions. Arab pirates dominated the Mediterranean and held fortified castles on the coast of Spain and southern France, from which they conducted raids into the hinterland. Hungarian warrior tribes ravaged Germany and northern Italy and reached as far west as the Loire valley. From the north the Vikings began plundering the coasts and river valleys of the rest of Europe. Gradually their expeditions became organized conquests, and Viking kingdoms were established in parts of England and northern France. The social institutions of Western Europe proved incapable of dealing with the invasions, and, as a result, in spite of great regional variations there are some common patterns in the way in which the distribution of tasks, land and goods developed after 800.

Many towns were plundered and burnt down. Long

distance trade became unreliable and each small area was thrown back on its own resources. No generally accepted coins were minted and such trade as there was, was mainly based on direct exchange.

Before the invasions the typical social unit was a kingdom. Large parts of the land were wild and uninhabited; the cultivated areas were divided into crown land, church land, private estates owned by lords and farms owned by free peasants. In theory a king raised tax on all land, and all free men were liable to do war service under their king. However, by the time a king raised an army the invaders had plundered and left. What was needed was a standing army of heavily armed horsemen, but the necessary equipment was much too expensive for most peasants; and the taxation system – based on payment in kind owing to the instability of money – did not permit the king himself to equip one. In this situation a form of remuneration which had its roots in antiquity, was gradually developed, and came to be a central institution over several centuries: the fief.

One way in which a fief could be created was by the king giving a part of the crown land in fief to an important military man, often a lord or a rich free peasant. The fiefholder became the lord of the peasants in the fief, and had the right to raise taxes and exercise legal authority. In return he swore allegiance to the king and undertook to take part in the defence of the realm against the enemies of the king and provide a certain number of fully equipped horsemen. Formally the fief still belonged to the king and reverted to him when the fiefholder died. The church was generally dependent on lay protection, so kings could often make fiefs of church land. This system of fiefs enabled kings to secure the equipment and upkeep of an army, and the legal and fiscal administration of the realm; but it also meant that large parts of the kingdom became semi-autonomous.

Another way of establishing a fief was for the king to exempt a lord from taxation if he in return agreed to take over the legal administration himself, swear loyalty to the king and equip and maintain a band of soldiers. This often took the form of the lord giving his land to the king and receiving it back as a hereditary fief with certain rights and duties. Fiefs which had originally been crown or church land soon became hereditary too, so the difference between them and the fiefs which had been free estates gradually disappeared, at least in many parts of Europe.

Great fiefholders, like their king, often gave parts of their fief in fief to their men in return for services and in order to secure continued loyalty and support. Parts of such subfiefs could in turn be given to knights lower in the military hierarchy, and so on. In this way the division of most of the cultivated land of the realm was modelled on a military hierarchy and the knights of the army became a nobility pledged to support the king, but with a large measure of autonomy as lords of their fiefs.

The lord's authority over his fief was based on the manor, and larger fiefs contained several of these. On each manor the lord had peasants under him. Typically a manor was divided into the lord's home farm (the demesne), and a village surrounded by peasant land. The peasants' land was usually divided into strips in the two or three open fields of the village. Some peasants were slaves belonging to the lord, working on the demesne or at the manor house. Other peasants were serfs, who belonged to the lord and worked on the demesne but were also given a farm to maintain themselves. Others were free tenants. They too had the right to cultivate a farm, and in return they had either to work on the demesne for a certain number of days or to pay rent in kind or in money. In varying degrees, free tenants had more personal freedom than serfs. In theory the lord of the manor would protect the village against attack and his peasants were free from royal taxation or conscription, though each farm might be obliged to muster foot soldiers for the lord. But becoming independent of the king meant becoming much more dependent on the lord, and generally the repression of serfs and free peasants increased considerably during the period of the invasions.

Free peasants who were not subject to any lord were also in a very precarious position. As the rest of the cultivated soil became exempt from taxation by being given in fief, an increasing burden of taxation fell on these peasants. They also needed protection both from invaders and from lords who wanted to take them over. In most of Europe this meant that the majority of freeholders were forced to subject themselves to a lord. Formally they gave him their lands and received them back as an hereditary tenancy, thereby achieving protection and exemption from taxation by the king, but at the price of having to work on the demesne or pay rent. Only in peripheral and inaccessible areas could substantial bodies of peasants survive as freeholders.

## The estate system

The fief system was thus a pyramidal structure with the king at the top and tenants, serfs and slaves at the base. Formally, the king was the supreme lord of all fiefs and all land ultimately belonged to him, but the fiefs gradually became hereditary and in some places one person might hold fiefs from more than one overlord. This meant that the fiefholder's oath became almost meaningless, and the real power of the king became very small. Single fiefs or even single manors were the largest social units which had any effective internal unity. Thus by far the greatest power was concentrated in the middle level of the pyramid. Vertical bonds of service and protection were replaced by horizontal bonds of common interest. In particular, what had been a disparate collection of lords separately responsible to the king, became a unified class or estate: the nobility.

A very strong social barrier and a decisive difference in status separated the nobility from the peasants. This barrier indicated a new form of the social division of labour. In earlier periods, many lords personally directed work on their lands and their peasants would join with them in military service when necessary. Now, the nobility monopolized the military and administrative tasks and was no longer involved with production, while the peasants stopped having to perform military and other tasks in their own right and were forced to concentrate on farm labour. This wider separation of nobility and peasants became increasingly a matter of birth. Mixed marriages between nobles and peasants became almost unthinkable and the opportunity to move from one level of the pyramid to another became rare indeed, though it never disappeared completely.

The nobility was in effective possession of the land. But within the institution of the fief, land could not have the status of exclusive or unconditional private property. In relation to any one plot of cultivated land, several people might have a right to say 'This land is mine'. A peasant could say it, meaning he was the tenant and had the right to cultivate it; a lord could say it, meaning he had a right to demand labour dues or rent from the tenant; a number of overlords could say it, meaning they had a right to demand military service of the lord; and the king could say it, meaning he had the right to demand military service from the fiefholders. No one had a total and exclusive right to a plot of land; no one had an unrestricted right to dispose of the plot as he thought fit; no one could sell or buy the plot without further ado. 'Mine' did not mean a universal 'not yours'.

The word 'feudalism' is derived from the Latin word 'feodum', a fief. Thus the word 'feudalism' literally means a society organized as a system of fiefs, with legal and political authority widely dispersed amongst persons with economic power. But it has become common to use the phrase more widely than this, in reference to any society where the greater part of social production is carried out by people who have to transfer part of their product to an hereditary estate of non-producers whose power depends on inherited privilege and force of arms. Payment could take the form of labour, or rent in kind, or money, or some combination of these.

The feudal mode of production is to be contrasted with the slave mode of production, where slaves belong to a lord who also owns everything they produce; and it differs from a mode of production based on the work of free peasants and free wage-labourers. In the period between 800 and 1000 the direct producers of Europe included slaves, dependent peasants and freeholders. But in the course of this period the feudal mode of production became more and more dominant because an increasing part of the total production was carried out by dependent peasants.

## Feudal expansion 1000-1300

By 1000, the invasions had more or less ceased and trade slowly began to improve. About 1050, population began to increase and the period from 1050 to about 1250 was one of growth for the European economy. The amount of cultivated land was greatly increased, as was agricultural productivity. Many new villages sprang up. The peasants who moved out from the old villages to cultivate the wilderness were normally tenants of a lord. But their situation was usually relatively free and they paid rent rather than working on the demesne. Commutations of labour dues into rent also took place in many of the old villages. Many slaves and serfs had the opportunity to buy their freedom and to become tenants or move to the towns.

The rise of trade and the regeneration of an internationally reliable currency led to the expansion of old towns and the growth of many new ones, often in the vicinity of fortified castles. Most of these were quite small, and served as the market town for a very limited area. In some parts of Europe, towns were subject to the nobility; in others they were immediately under the king. Normally they had a charter which gave them a trading monopoly in most products within a certain area, and a certain amount of autonomy in return for an annual duty. Some large towns, mainly in northern Italy and southern Germany, were based on long distance trade, and a few of these were autonomous city states.

The merchants usually dominated the town council – the internal government of the towns. They were normally organized into one or more guilds with a monopoly of trade in certain products. Directly or indirectly the guilds controlled prices and the quality of goods in order to ensure that all their members would get a fair share of the trade. Inevitably prices varied with supply and demand, but the guilds took many precautions to avoid price competition. Admission to a guild was controlled by the guild itself, and guilds gave financial support to needy members and their children.

Most of the work – building, the production of clothes and the processing of food – was done by the peasant families in the villages, but the expansion of trade extended the division of labour, with full-time artisans like carpenters, weavers, smiths and bakers setting up business in the towns. These producers were typically organized into corporations which determined rules for apprenticeship and entry qualifications. In some towns they could fix their own prices, but often this was done by the council which was dominated by the merchants' guild.

In the towns, the members of the guilds and corporations, together with their dependants, had greater personal freedom than the peasants on the manors. But they were nevertheless organized in a hierarchical, status-determined system and each merchant house or workshop was organized hierarchically with a master, journeymen and apprentices – who usually belonged to the household of the master and were subject to his authority.

Trade with the outside world was largely subject to the tolls and duties imposed by the nobility and it took place in a regulated, rather than a free, market.

During the invasions the church was weak and disorganized but its power and independence grew in the centuries after 1000. It exerted great influence as an omnipresent factor with a monopoly in the education of the few who did receive an education and in the communication and interpretation of news and ideas for the whole of society. Internally the structure of the church was hier-archical, with village priests on the bottom level of the pyramid, the pope on the top and higher church officers, like bishops and archbishops, in between. The costs of the church were covered by the tithes which all peasants had to pay, but apart from these, bishops were also remuner-ated by holding fiefs. After a series of struggles over the issue they were appointed by the church itself rather than by the king. This was a clear indication of the growing strength of the church. However, the church was part of a hierarchical society, so, whoever appointed them, bishops were usually younger sons of noble families.

In Germany and Italy the fiefholders were highly inde-pendent of the crown, and the towns were often independ-ent too. In the rest of Western Europe there was a balance of power between crown and nobility, and this gave the kings a better chance of exercising centralized control over their realm. By various fiscal means, and by extending royal demesnes and increasing the income from them, kings gradually became able to finance standing armies and so secure some degree of independence from the nobility.

In England the king became especially strong because of the highly systematic feudal order established by William the Conqueror after the invasion of 1066. Every-one who held the land in fief had to be sworn in by the king even if he held it as a subject from another fiefholder; the lands of great noblemen were widely dispersed to prevent them from becoming small principalities; and the towns were directly controlled by the crown. Despite all this, however, the power of the king was far from absolute. Before accession to the throne the king, in England and in the rest of Europe, had to agree to a coronation charter limiting his power in many ways.

So, by about 1250 a relatively stable, highly stratified

social structure had crystallized. The realm consisted of three social orders: those who prayed for the realm, those who fought for it, and those who produced food and other necessities. Occasionally, fiefs could be sold by overlords when vacant but there was certainly no free market in land. Conditional property rights to land were, generally, reserved for the noble families. There was no free labour market and the great bulk of production was carried out by dependent producers who were legally bound in various ways to their lords and masters. There was a market for the distribution of products and services, but it was not free.

## Thinking about feudal society

These feudal institutions formed the background and starting point for any thirteenth-century man or woman thinking about social life. For all of them tradition was the main arbiter of right and wrong. The fact that a certain pattern had been followed for a long time, or from time immemorial, constituted the strongest possible argument in its favour. Changes were avoided or regarded with suspicion – though the rather short memory of a largely illiterate culture made greater changes possible than this emphasis on tradition might make one expect. If something happened once, it was well on the way to becoming a custom. So anyone who got away with some action thereby gained what virtually amounted to a right to do it again.

Local peasant riots occurred from time to time but usually when some action of the lord or his bailiffs was regarded as a breach of custom. Revolts against custom or against serfdom as such did not occur. The lords had the military power to crush riots, but for long periods they did not need to resort to force in order to uphold their privileges. It was taken for granted that some people were noble by birth and others serfs, just as the division of labour between men and women in the village was taken as part of the natural order of things. The authority of custom was fully backed up by the world view of the church.

For centuries the cornerstone of the church's social thought had been the belief that institutions of subjection were a punishment for Adam and Eve's fall and the consequent corruption of all their offspring. By the grace of God, kings were set above other people in order to exterminate evil. But, gradually, a rather different conception gained acceptance: the view that the basic features of the feudal social order were a result of divine ordinance and not just a punishment for human disobedience. In this view, the subjection of people to their masters, lords and king was natural and legitimate provided it kept within certain limits – otherwise it was unnatural and illegitimate. This view found its full expression in the social philosophy of Thomas Aquinas, whose great work the *Summa Theologica* (1265-73) had become the official teaching of the church by the end of the thirteenth century.

## The social philosophy of Aquinas

For Aquinas, the fundamental truth was that the world was created by God as an organized whole. The order of the universe was an expression of the eternal law of God which ruled the whole of creation – rocks, plants, animals, humans, angels and archangels, the earth, the moon, the sun and the stars. It prescribed the position of everything in the great order of all things, and it prescribed the rules specific to each position. When a stone fell to earth, it was in accordance with the rules for lifeless things whose proper place was on the surface of the earth. When a man performed his duty, it was in accordance with the rules for rational beings. God was completely rational, and the more rational a person, the nearer he approached to God. Being rational, man – and to a smaller degree, woman – had the capacity to follow the law of God consciously, unlike a stone which, in falling to earth, acts without understanding. On the other hand, man might err and follow his animal instincts instead of his reason. In this case he would be betraying his position in the universe, and would be liable to the punishment of God.

So the social order, for Aquinas, was part of the order of the universe. God had created a world ordered according to degrees of rationality and perfection, and society, too, was created as a hierarchy ordered according to degrees of rationality. Generally, men were considered more rational than women and so should rule them; likewise parents were more rational than children, and so on. In general the more rational should rule over the less rational for the good of one and all and for the glory of God. The family was likened to a human body with the father as the head or the organ of reason. He was responsible for organizing things for the benefit of the whole body. This required the individual members of the body to obey orders unquestioningly – a hand or foot could not judge what was in the best interest of the whole. However the head should not forget that it was connected with the rest of the body and dependent upon it. The peasants on a manor were like children of the lord of the manor, or like the members of a body of which he was the head. In the realm as a whole, the king was like the father or head of all, and in the final analysis kings had to obey God, the king of kings, the loving father and the world-reason itself.

God was one, his reason was one, and his plan for the universe was one. So nothing could be independent of the rest of the universe or be understood apart from creation as a whole.

But how, according to Aquinas, could one know the contents of God's plan? The eternal law of God went far beyond the limits of human understanding. It governed nature and the supernatural, the heavens and the realm of the angels. Parts of it had been revealed in the Bible; and in the Ten Commandments and the Sermon on the Mount human beings had the most authoritative expressions of their duty. Whether or not one understood the reason for

these revealed laws one had to put trust in their correctness and follow them. But in addition to such direct revela-
tions of God's law, human beings could grasp small port-
ions of it by making use of their limited reason. Thus in the
field of natural philosophy, human beings could achieve
some insight into the workings of inanimate nature although, according to Aquinas, Aristotle had already gone
about as far in this direction as it was possible to go.
Similarly, in social philosophy human reason was able to
discover proofs of rules against such practices as lying,
stealing and disobedience, cheating in trade or charging
interest on loans. These rules, it was thought, could be
established by natural means, without relying on revelation. Aquinas called the part of God's eternal law which
human reason was capable of understanding and proving
'natural law' or 'natural right'. These rules laid down
duties and goals for all human beings in accordance with
their place in the social hierarchy, rules which were taken
to be valid at all times and places, independent of human
institutions.

The parts of the eternal law which could be known
either by natural law or by divine revelation were very
general in character and needed specification and elabor-
ation in order to be applicable to concrete situations. This
mediation was the responsibility of the rational and the
learned, of the church and the civil authorities. The positive, humanly given church law and secular law was, and
had to be, an adaptation of the eternal law. No one could
escape the punishment of God, but in the transgressor's
own interest, the civil authorities had to try to ensure that
all transgressions were punished and atoned for in this life
rather than in the next.

The powers that be are ordained of God. Whosoever
therefore resisteth the power, resisteth the ordinance of
God; and they that resist shall receive to themselves
damnation. For rulers are not a terror to good works,
but to the evil. Wilt thou then not be afraid of the

power? do that which is good, and thou shalt have
praise of the same: for he is the minister of God to thee
for good. But if thou do that which is evil, be afraid; for
he beareth not the sword in vain: for he is the minister of
God, a revenger to execute wrath upon him that doeth
evil.                                                                          *Romans 13* vv 1-4

Aquinas's world view, and his account of law and
reason could obviously be used to justify enormous legal
and economic inequalities; but only up to a point. Natural
law was open to many interpretations but it did have a
content which set limits to the justifiable exercise of power.
No lord had unlimited and unconditional power over his
subjects; even the greatest of feudal lords would eventually
be judged by the supreme head of the world. Property
rights were not unconditional either. People who stole
took something which was not theirs, and this was obviously against natural law, and besides, the scripture
revealed God's Eighth Commandment, 'Thou shalt not
steal'; but under certain circumstances it might still be
right to steal – for instance starving peasants might justi-
fiably raid the granaries of a lord if he refused to carry out
his own duty to help those in need.

A people had the right to resist a prince who clearly
violated natural law and, in the case of a prince making
laws contrary to the revealed law, the people had not only
a right but a duty to revolt. However, this should not be
taken too literally. Aquinas did not believe that it was for a
peasant to decide whether a prince was transgressing the
law. The church had a monopoly in interpreting the
revealed law, and the interpretation of natural law had to
be left to those most fully endowed with reason, who were,
as it happened, also part of the church. Thus the right to
resist and the duty to revolt really meant the duty to follow
the church rather than the king if they should disagree.

Natural law had both moral and economic implications. Morally it meant that the final criterion for the
rightness and goodness of an action was that it accorded

with the law of God. Such actions – or rather the avoidance of actions contrary to the law of God – would lead to redemption and eternal life. You should follow the laws of God even if this went against your inclinations and destroyed your happiness; you ought to mould your feelings so that you would feel pleasure in obeying the law – always bearing in mind that happiness in this life is a very small thing compared to eternal torment in Hell.

Economically, natural law implied that the just and right price of a product was determined in advance of the interaction of buyers and sellers in the market. The just price, according to Aquinas, was made up of the costs of production plus a payment to the producer in accordance with his status. Thus, though supply and demand might alter the actual price, they had nothing to do with the just price.

A special case of selling above the just price was taking interest on a loan. To charge interest was to commit the sin of usury. To expect to get more in return than was lent, to ask for something in return for nothing, was obviously against natural law. However, Aquinas thought it might be fair to demand interest in recompense for any losses suffered as a result of not having the money, and this left a loophole for the justification of moderate interest charges.

The society in which Aquinas lived was not the harmonious hierarchy implied by his social philosophy; in fact when he argued that usury was a sin or that it was wrong to sell things for more than their just price, he was arguing against what he knew to be current practices – practices which he saw as threatening the stability of the whole system.

The basic concepts which Aquinas employed in his account of the order of the universe referred to mutual but unequal ties of dependence between the elements of a hierarchy. These concepts had been developing throughout the period which saw the rise of the nobility, the decline of royal power and the elimination of peasant freedom. When these concepts were applied to society,

they made the actual rule of the lords seem just and
reasonable and in accordance with the divine and natural
order of things – unless it was in open conflict with the
interests of the church.

# 3

# The crisis of feudalism and the social philosophy of Hobbes

## The crisis of the fourteenth century and its effects 1300-1500

About 1300, feudal expansion came to an end. Exhaustion of the soil and the generally poorer quality of the as yet uncultivated land were amongst the reasons for this, and a deterioration in climate and a series of very bad harvests may also have contributed to it. From the middle of the fourteenth century the crisis was greatly deepened by a series of plague epidemics, which cut the population of Europe by at least a quarter.

The immediate effects of the plague were most devastating in the densely populated towns, which responded by trying to entice peasants to come and settle and by seeking wider and securer trade monopolies from the crown. (In northern Germany, in fact, the mainly independent towns formed a league, the Hanseatic League, which effectively controlled mutual competition and excluded outside competition.)

In the long term, however, the plagues had much more far-reaching structural effects in the countryside than in the towns. The first reaction of the nobility was to demand more labour or higher rents from the peasants who survived, and to try and stop them from settling in the towns. In Europe east of the Elbe, this intensification of feudal repression was successful: towns were fewer and less powerful, and the nobility was stronger because it could rely on the crown to enforce laws which bound peasants to the manor where they were born. But in Western Europe, especially England and France, no such intensification took place. Towns were more numerous and the ranks of the nobility were weakened by plague, war and internal strife. This strengthened the crown, and enabled it to augment its income by selling vacant fiefdoms to rich merchants who were prepared to pay handsomely, since landholding was still the key to influence and power. Attempts to intensify the exploitation of the peasantry, however, led to a number of peasant revolts which, though repressed, succeeded in heading off direct attacks on peasants' rights from the crown and the nobility.

This meant that the nobility of Western Europe had to seek new ways of maintaining their income. Their first reaction had been to resort to the stick; when this failed they tried the carrot. Peasants were encouraged to commute their labour dues into money rent and lords could give up demesne farming altogether, and lease their demesne lands as well. This yielded higher rents, and enabled the lords to dispense with a staff of bailiffs and overseers. The lords themselves could then concentrate on getting further income by exploiting court service and various monopolies to which their noble rank might entitle them. This was the most common pattern in France and in some parts of England. In other parts of England, the lord tried to enlarge the demesne and to switch from arable to sheep farming, which required less labour.

The crisis of the fourteenth century led to many more transfers of land and much greater social mobility than had been seen in the previous century. The nobility was weakened and the crown and the towns became stronger. On some manors hired hands and day-labourers began to replace the labour of tenants. This was a non-feudal way of organizing production, in that it did not depend on applying legal pressure to the producers. They were paid for working rather than obliged to work or to hand over part of their own produce; and they were subject to the lord's power only for their working hours. However, by far the largest part of production was still carried out by tenants paying customary rents to the lord of the manor, and the traditional, hereditary privileges of the feudal nobility were still guaranteed by the crown.

## New prosperity 1500-1600

The feudal order had been shaken, and the structural changes which had already begun accelerated quickly as the economic decline was reversed at the end of the fifteenth century. By this time, population and trade were growing rapidly, and towns were expanding and creating a new demand for agricultural products. At the same time there was an influx of gold and silver from America, and improved techniques of ore processing were discovered. The consequent abundance of bullion led to a fall in the value of money and an increase in money prices: inflation. The fact that prices tended to increase over an extended period of time was an advantage for those who had goods to sell, but not for those who had none or who had fixed money incomes.

In Western Europe the lords who had given up demesne farming found that their money incomes from ordinary long-term leases were lagging seriously behind their customery expenses. This forced them to seek ways of supplementing their income, and if possible of increasing rents. The tenants, on the other hand, with products to sell and land in leasehold for life could improve their position considerably. The more land tenants held, the better their chances of producing a surplus which could be marketed. This income could then be used to rent more land, or to improve land, buildings or stock. Smaller tenants became correspondingly poorer, and many of them were forced to become day-labourers for other tenants at least for part of the year. Thus the rich peasants grew richer, and the poor became poorer, often giving up their small landholdings and becoming full-time day-labourers with only a cottage and a small garden. Alternatively, they moved into the towns – which consequently expanded even more and needed to buy agricultural produce in larger quantities at ever higher prices.

On those manors where the lord was often absent, and where all dues were paid in money or in kind, the status of the tenants was no longer servile. By and large the lord's land was cultivated by free tenants and day-labourers, but exclusive property rights were still not clearly defined, cultivation was generally done in common, and the lords retained a number of privileges.

In Eastern Europe, lords who had kept their demesne and succeeded in forcing more labour from their peasants, profited enormously from inflation and the growing opportunities to sell grain to cities in the West. The towns of Eastern Europe were relatively weak, which gave the peasants less chance of marketing their own products. This, combined with their servile status, meant that their situation did not improve much; no class of wealthy tenants appeared and very few peasants had the opportunity to leave the villages.

Those lords in the West – mainly in England – who had kept their demesnes or even extended them were in a fortunate position. On some of their manors the common land had already been enclosed: some of it, that is, was divided into parts, each attached to a farm, but most of it was added to the demesne. On others they tried to persuade the villagers to agree to enclosures. The new lords, especially merchants who had paid high prices for estates and titles, looked upon their manors as investments and were eager to increase their returns. Instead of wishing to be self-sufficient and to spend their income on luxurious consumption, the new nobles were more interested than their predecessors in systematic production of commodities for the market. They sought to cut production costs and to re-invest part of the profit in improvements to the land and other means of production.

Enclosure was often in the interest of large tenants. For smaller ones, however, such new land as they might acquire was very unlikely to make up for the loss of grazing, hunting and wood-gathering rights on the commons. Many of them became day-labourers, or had to move to the towns.

On many of the enclosed manors, the main marketable product was wool. In the fifteenth century most English wool was processed abroad (mainly in Flanders). But English merchants (many of them also lords of manors) began to have the wool made into cloth themselves, and they marketed it both abroad and at home. Often the cloth was woven by peasants and their families as a way of supplementing their meagre income. In theory they bought the wool from the merchant and then sold him the cloth; in practice the merchant often supplied them with both the wool and the loom and an advance payment, and then deducted the price and rent for these from the price paid for the cloth. For the merchant the one great advantage in this system – the 'putting-out' system – was that he could bypass the weavers' corporations in the towns, and deal separately with unorganized and constantly debt-ridden producers. Large fortunes were made in this trade.

In the traditional, feudal relations of lord to tenant, the prosperity of the lord depended on the difference in their legal status. The lord had legal authority over his tenants so that he could punish them if they did not do what they were customarily bound to do. On the other hand, the lord himself was bound by custom to some extent, and he could not easily evict a tenant. In the case of relations between landlord and day-labourer, or merchant and weaver, the employer had no legal authority over his employees, but neither was he bound to let them have land. The tenant was dependent on a particular lord but had at least some land to live off. The day-labourer was not dependent on any particular employer and was free to go wherever he liked, but nevertheless he relied heavily on there being an employer to give him work since he had to buy everything he needed in the market. Under the threat of being sacked, day-labourers worked with much greater intensity and discipline than tenants working either for themselves or on the demesne.

## The English Revolutions and continental absolutism 1600-1700

The old nobility of Western Europe was generally in economic decline, and was heavily dependent on the crown which upheld such privileges as their exclusive right to lucrative government offices, and, in many parts of Europe, their right to demand tolls and duties on trade passing through their territory. In all of this, the interests of the old nobility clashed with those of the merchants and of the new nobility, who, especially in England, were achieving an economic power which was largely independent of feudal privileges. The merchants needed to be able to forecast prices, and were always anxious to cut costs; but feudal tolls and duties were an expensive nuisance to them, as was the often arbitrary and corrupt use of government positions by noblemen which made all forecasts highly uncertain.

The old nobility, in Western Europe at least, no longer played a crucial military role, and so they could not offer much to the king who protected their privileges. Large merchants and modernizing lords, on the other hand, could offer the king loans, and the economic security of this group was growing anyway through their purchase of titles and land from the crown. In England and Northern Europe, large tracts of monastery and church land were confiscated during the Reformation, and most of this land, along with the accompanying titles, was sold to merchants and modernizing lords.

The economic strength of this new sector of the upper class was greatest in England. Here its political influence was exerted through the House of Commons, where it was able to work against both the old nobility and the king. In the first English revolution in the 1640s, this new upper class took over the power of the state, that is the right to act on behalf of everyone in the land. The king fled but was later caught and put on trial – an act without precedent. He was found guilty of crimes against the people, sentenced to death in the name of the people and executed in 1649.

This revolution abolished certain feudal institutions which had made the property rights of landowners dependent on the crown, but it did not interfere with the feudal rights of landlords over their tenants. The monarchy was restored in 1660, but following the second English Revolution, the 'Glorious Revolution' of 1688, the monarchy was restricted to governing in accordance with the wishes of the new upper class, as represented by the House of Commons.

On the continent things were different. The general weakening of the economic position of the nobility made it both possible and necessary for kings to create or strengthen centralized state agencies, and they often did so with the active support of rich merchants. In many places traditional checks on royal power, such as systems of representation by the estates, or coronation charters, were abolished. Regionally unified national states with absolute monarchs became the norm.

Absolutism had not arisen in England because a powerful coalition between merchants (or rather the urban bourgeoisie) and the modernizing sectors of the nobility had been formed, and they had no need of an absolute monarch. No similar coalition was possible on the continent largely because of the greater homogeneity of the nobility who clung to privilege as the only source of income befiting their status. An exception was the Netherlands, the most urbanized region in Europe, which had gained independence as a republic as early as 1581.

Absolutism was a form of state which upheld feudal relations of production after the military and other functions of the landholding but non-producing class had disappeared. But absolutist states also had to encourage non-feudal forms of trade and manufacture; and to this extent they did limit the power of the old nobility.

A similar systematic ambivalence characterized the typical economic policies of European states well into the eighteenth or even nineteenth century. These policies, which can be grouped together under the heading 'mercantilism', can be seen from one point of view as the application at a national level of the traditional policy of the self-sufficiency of the manor. According to mercantilist doctrine, the state should aim to possess as much gold and silver as possible because possession of these metals gives the state the ability to raise an army. To achieve this power a positive balance of payments with other nations is needed. This implies regulating foreign trade in order to protect national production, and perhaps also dismantling internal barriers to trade, such as feudal tolls and duties.

Merchants were generally in favour of these policies, which both enabled them to expand their markets locally and protected them from foreign competition. They did not demand free trade, but simply wanted to replace regulations which blocked their own advance with ones which blocked the advance of others.

## The Reformation and the Scientific Revolution

As early as the fourteenth century, certain theologians had criticized the view – articulated by Aquinas – that human reason partly coincides with the rationality of God, with its corollary that natural law is a law given by God but known and understood by human beings. The critics claimed that the gulf between God and humans was utterly unbridgeable. The rationality and goodness of God, they argued, was totally beyond the grasp of human thought, and it would be blasphemous to think otherwise. The purpose of life on earth was to earn eternal life, but human reason could not work out how this was to be done. It was irrelevant: each individual was alone before God, a sinner who in fear and anguish could do no more than hope in humility to be touched by God's grace. But if God was so far removed from human beings then there could be no mediators, neither priests, pope, nor king. All human beings, however noble or base, were equal before God. God was elevated so far above this world, that no one could claim to have any understanding of God's will.

This more exalted conception of God was among the theoretical preconditions of the Scientific Revolution within astronomy and mechanics. If human reason had no direct access to divine plans, then people would have to find out about the world by trusting their own logic and their own senses without relying on revelation and ancient opinions. But careful observations of the movements of heavenly bodies, of the acceleration of falling bodies, or of the circulation of blood through the human body, became increasingly difficult to explain within the old framework of a hierarchical world order with things at different levels each striving for their own kind of perfection. In fact, events of the most diverse types seemed to be describable in mathematical terms and to be explicable as effects of earlier events acting as causes (mechanical explanation) rather than in terms of an ideal state towards which they

were all striving (teleological explanation). This crucial
scientific movement was greatly stimulated by the practical use of the results of the new science in navigation,
surveying, artillery and other technical fields.

The new conception of God was not only more exalted
but also more personal. The invention of printing, the
spread of literacy and the translation of the Bible into
modern languages allowed many people, including peasants and artisans, to believe in the possibility of direct
contact with God. This led to the rise of a vast number of
sects and congregations in opposition to the official Catholic church. In many places this in turn led to rebellions by
peasants and by whole towns and cities who wished to live
by the Bible without the intercession of lords and bishops.
Most of these rebellions were brutally crushed, and those
which were not were tolerated mainly because some
prince utilized them to strengthen his own power both
economically (through confiscation of monastery and
church land) and politically (by eliminating the allegiance
of the church to a foreign power. In many countries the
head of state also became the head of the church). In these
cases the sects were integrated into a reformed church and
their independence was eroded comparatively quickly.
Discontent with this development was one of the important motivations for the increasing emigration to the New
World.

The disintegration of the unity of the church and the
change from a teleological to a mechanical cosmology
made new theories of the legitimate bases of political
power necessary. Some of the popular movements
amongst German peasants in the sixteenth century, and
some radical groups active in the first English Revolution,
had clearly-formulated democratic ideas about self-
governing, egalitarian communities in which men and
women could live together as brothers and sisters in the
love of God. However, the absolute monarchs and the
official reformed churches adhered to and propagated the
view that kings were kings by the grace of God. This view

raised kings more decisively above the rest of society than did the view of Aquinas. The exaltation of God at the expense of mediators, like popes and bishops, was parallelled in the exaltation of the king at the expense of mediators like lords. New powers had arisen, but it was still believed that 'the powers that be are ordained by God'.

## The social philosophy of Hobbes

Thomas Hobbes, who was in exile in Paris as a Royalist during most of the first English Revolution, gave a very different justification of absolutism. Although he made use of some theological arguments, his account did not depend on any religious assumptions at all (*Leviathan*, 1651).

A natural right, for Hobbes, was a right which human beings would have even if there were no human social institutions. Aquinas would have accepted this definition too, but whereas Aquinas conceived that human beings in this imaginary 'state of nature' would still be positioned within a hierarchically ordered system of duties and rights, Hobbes thought they would be subject only to natural laws in the sense of the new natural sciences, laws such as the law of gravitation and the mechanical law that a moving body will continue its movement unless prevented by external interference. For him, all life consisted of vital motion: the working of the heart, breathing and digesting. These movements likewise tended to continue unless prevented from doing so, and rational animals were motivated by an aversion to everything likely to stop these vital movements. In a state of nature, everyone would therefore do whatever they thought would secure their own survival, irrespective of whether this would harm others, or be contrary to some divine law. This, for Hobbes, was the fundamental natural right; in the final analysis it would explain all human action and provide the only possible basis for legitimating or criticizing human institutions.

Aquinas thought that differences in strength and

rationality produced a natural hierarchy among human beings, but for Hobbes, all human beings were equal: individual variations in strength and rationality were negligible from the only point of view that mattered: survival. Everyone was vulnerable: even the strongest had to sleep from time to time, and a child could easily kill a slumbering giant. Differences in reason were even less significant than differences in strength. After all, who ever heard anyone complain that he had too little reason? Thus, in a state of nature as Hobbes conceived it, no one could be sure of not being killed or robbed of their food or mates. The state of nature was a state of war. There was nothing to stop people from killing, wounding or robbing others. In it there was not much point in cultivating land because it was uncertain who would reap the harvest. Therefore, Hobbes felt, there was obviously an overwhelming need to escape from a state of nature.

Thus, for Hobbes the idea of natural right led to that of a natural law commanding human beings to set limits to their natural right to do whatever they wanted. Natural law would therefore require me to give up my right to harm others provided that they also gave up their right to harm me. But, unless I could be sure that others would actually refrain from harming me it would be stupid for me to give up my right to harm them. Therefore it would be necessary not only for everyone to enter into a contract renouncing the right to harm others, but also for there to be a power which could guarantee that anyone who broke the contract by harming another would be hurt even more in return. Thus, as Hobbes saw it, human nature required human beings to subject themselves to a power which could enforce rules forbidding people to harm others, and establishing and protecting property rights. If they did, then organized social life would come to an end and human beings would relapse into a state of nature.

The basis of a secure and organized society, for Hobbes, was a contract by which each individual member of society transferred his or her right to harm others to a particular person or group of persons, on condition that everyone else did the same. The person or group which was thereby endowed with an exclusive right to harm people was called the sovereign, the supreme power. In theory, the sovereign could be male or female, an individual or a group; but in fact, Hobbes argued, it was usually best if the sovereign was one man. The sovereign was not a party to the contract: he possessed all legislative, judicial and executive power, and was above the law. This followed from the fact that there could not be anyone with the power to punish any of his actions, and without the possibility of punishment it was meaningless to speak of law or crime. Even if the sovereign actually gained power by conquering the land and subjecting its inhabitants to his rule, they could, according to Hobbes, be considered to have voluntarily entered a mutual contract to accept his absolute rule, since their only alternative was death. Thus, within Hobbes's philosophy, the idea of the total freedom of the individual in nature is made to imply the need to accept complete subjection in society. In terms of the society of Hobbes's time, this meant, amongst other things, that even those participating in a post-feudal mode of production, working ceaselessly to enrich themselves through trade and manufacture, would have to accept the power of the absolutist state.

Royal propaganda might claim that the king ruled by the grace of God; Hobbes, by contrast, saw him as elected by the people out of a fear of reversion to a state of nature. This justification of absolutism made the relation between the sovereign and his subjects a matter of pure power, with no element of fatherly love or wisdom. But in spite of the enormous and uncontrolled power it ascribed to the sovereign, it did not promise unconditional allegiance from the subjects. If a king was not strong enough to uphold law and order or defend the country against invaders, then in Hobbes's system there was nothing to stop his subjects from deserting him: if a king was so weak that he could not guarantee his subjects a better chance of survival than they would have had in a state of nature, then his position was untenable.

In Hobbes's philosophy, individuals became subjects by giving up their right to harm others, but it would be contrary to natural right for anyone to give up the right to self-defence. No human law could oblige a person to acquiesce in being harmed. The sovereign would try to punish anyone who broke the law, but the criminal would also have the right to resist: he could not be obliged to give himself up, to give incriminating evidence or to walk voluntarily to the gallows: in other words, once a crime had been committed there was a state of war between the criminal and the sovereign.

Hobbes also thought that smaller groups, like the family, were based on a contract between free individuals. A newborn child was immediately subject to the natural law that it must do everything within its power to survive. But, as its power was very small, it had to enter a silent contract pledging obedience to its mother or whoever fed it. Since the mother was often (though not necessarily) dependent on a man, the child would be indirectly subject to the mother's husband. (Whether he was also the child's father was irrelevant for Hobbes. Biological parenthood in itself did not confer any obligations or rights, and in any case one could never be really sure who was the father of a child. The only relevant question was: who supports the child?) Thus, for Hobbes the family was not bound together by love and tenderness or by the natural superiority of the male sex: it was the arena of a power struggle in which everyone sought protection from the strong or command over the weak. The relation between a master and his servant was also a matter of a contract, of a rather indeterminate kind which made the servant himself, the fruits of his labour, and his possessions subject to the rule of the master.

For Hobbes, all contracts were entered into by parties who were basically equal in the sense that the difference in natural power between them was too small and impermanent to be the basis of a binding relationship of dominance between them. Nevertheless the power would naturally differ to some extent, and the whole point of contracts was to create a stable, social inequality by making the temporarily weaker party agree to the domination of the stronger. People could be efficiently bound only if they bound themselves. And even if the stronger party actually forced the weaker party to agree to the contract both parties were still, according to Hobbes, entering into the contract voluntarily.

For Aquinas, society, like nature, was hierarchically structured by God. To Hobbes, differences of rank were the outcome of competition between naturally equal human beings in the framework of the laws laid down by the sovereign. Human beings had no value or status prior to this competition. Social life was a sort of market-place with people trying to sell themselves as dearly as possible. No one could be noble in the state of nature, but the sovereign could select certain individuals and constitute them as a nobility. Hence nobles owed their status to the sovereign rather than to their 'blue blood' or their supposed God-given abilities. For Hobbes, the ideal sovereign was someone like William the Conqueror, who created a highly systematic form of feudalism in which no one was likely to forget that the real power in society flowed from the sovereign.

There is a similar difference between Hobbes and Aquinas in their treatment of economic value. For Aquinas the value of a product had nothing to do with human transactions, and natural prices ought to correspond to these values (see p.19). For Hobbes, however, a product had no value except in relation to transactions in the market. The price paid for a product in the market was the just price and the natural value of the product. The value could be determined objectively by seeing how much it could be sold for, but the value would depend only on the strength of the desires of potential purchasers.

The point of departure for Hobbes was the lonely individual, desperately trying to create some order in a cold, threatening and incalculable world. For Aquinas, the orderliness of creation could be taken for granted, and individuals had only to find and fill their position within that order. For Hobbes, society was an artificial device designed to advance the fundamental interests of all, a mechanism working by the interaction of basically independent individual parts. But the mechanism could break down if the friction between the parts became too great – for instance if people forgot that their interest in peace must always be greater than their interest in self-aggrandizement. For Aquinas, society was natural, created by God not humans; it did not make sense to speak of it as an artificial device set up to serve the interests of individuals. Individuals and interests existed only within an orderly society.

It is common and basically correct to characterize Hobbes's social philosophy as mechanical, in contrast to the organic philosophy of Aquinas. For Aquinas everyone had an obligation towards the society of which he or she was a part. For Hobbes, no one had any natural obligation to society, no one naturally owed anyone anything, and the only obligations were ones people freely entered into in order to serve their own interest. This view is the basic tenet of all forms of liberalism. But liberalism in this sense is not, as it is sometimes taken to be, the opposite of authoritariansim. For instance, Hobbes's liberalism would support quite violent 'illiberal' interventions into the personal and political freedom of individuals on the basis of the natural right of anyone to do whatever was necessary for personal survival.

Hobbes's philosophy provides a framework within which absolutist conclusions can be deduced from premises which are the cornerstones of liberalism. Human beings are equal but unsocial by nature, but they decide, in their own interest, to let the state force them to be social by setting one individual above all others and allowing the sovereign to create differences of rank in society. Hobbesian individuals are acquisitive, ambitious, and not by nature obedient: to this extent, they have the makings of capitalists. However, the society which Hobbes envisaged was, in fact, far from being a capitalist society: in it, production was carried out by dependent producers rather than by wage-earners and freeholders, and private property was not secure either – the sovereign had the right to confiscate it and the poor had the right to steal if they were starving. For Hobbes, capitalism would threaten to destroy social institutions in a civil war (which would be a state of nature). The only solution was the monopolization of all power by the state, reducing both bourgeoisie and nobility to complete dependence on the crown, which was the sole fount of peace and guarantor of the stability of the hierarchy of social differences. Hobbes saw people as basically capitalist by nature but argued that they were a danger to themselves, so that a rational consideration of their risks would show that they ought to prefer a systematized, feudal form of society.

# 4

# Early capitalism: its proponents and opponents

## England 1689-1780

From 1689 onwards the modernized class of landowning traders and trading landowners was solidly in power in England. Most government officials were recruited from this group, and legislation and foreign policy were determined in their interest.

In the course of the eighteenth century the remnants of the feudal system of production were abolished throughout the English countryside. Enclosure became the rule rather than the exception. Commonland was divided into private landholdings, and open field cultivation ceased. This was clearly to the advantage of the bigger landowners and leaseholding farmers who, by employing day-labourers, could supply the expanding market for agricultural products, and produce enough surplus to improve their soil, crops and livestock, thus producing even more for the market. But smaller freeholders, copyholders or tenants were gradually forced to sell their land or to give up their tenancies. Thus, through a long process reaching back to the crisis of the fourteenth century or even earlier, most of the land of England became the private property of a relatively small number of families. Cultivation was organized by tenant farmers who rented large farms on short leases, and labour was performed by day-labourers with no rights in the land and no political influence whatsoever.

The feudal system of property, which gave no one exclusive rights in the land, the most important factor of production, had been gradually replaced by capitalist institutions which assigned exclusive private rights to the owner of each piece of land, leaving the vast majority of the people without any property at all and with nothing to sell but their labour power. This process greatly increased agricultural productivity. It also enormously increased the size and the importance of the market, forcing nearly everyone to depend very heavily on it.

During the eighteenth century, the network of canals was greatly extended. This drastically reduced the transport costs of coal and iron and so increased the importance of mining. This also worked to the advantage of landowners, who had the right to any minerals found on their land.

Within textile production the putting-out system was gradually being supplemented by that of manufacture, with the merchant concentrating the work under one roof, thus cutting transport costs, gaining certain economies of scale, and being able to control and discipline the workers to ensure a constant output, instead of being subject to the whims of the individual worker who could stop working when he felt like it (or if better work presented itself). Some use was made of water-power in the textile factories, but human muscle was still the main moving force. Industry in the modern sense of the word did not exist until the 1780s.

The general view of society which members of the new

ruling class took for granted was highly individualistic. Everyone, they thought, was the architect of his own fortunes which, of course, meant that those who had high office and great wealth had them because of their personal talent, skill and diligence. The new ruling class was against the hereditary privileges of the old nobility, but they defended the right to inherit economic wealth, which obviously gave their own heirs great advantages.

This view of society was an optimistic and rationalistic form of liberalism. It was characterized by the belief that a real increase in the wealth of the nation could be achieved if all hindrances to the rational and self-interested plans of the members of the ruling class were removed and state policies geared to their needs. The state existed for the sake of its citizens, and not the other way round. Popular protests against the greed of the rich and mighty, their encroachments on long standing traditional rights and their tendency to treat human relations in terms of the market were not uncommon, but severe penalties were dealt out to those who transgressed against the new laws of property. At the same time the liberal view of society was being widely and efficiently propagated through new channels of communication, chiefly the press. Public opinion – open debate among educated men – became a social force and the new common ground of discussion was the sanctity of property.

## The social philosophy of Locke

A philosophical articulation of this optimistic liberalism was offered by John Locke at the time of the second English revolution in 1688 (*Two Treatises of Government*, 1690). Locke's liberalism was much more popular with the bourgeoisie than Hobbes's defence of absolutism had been.

For Hobbes, natural right was everyone's unlimited right to do anything for the sake of self-preservation, but there was no duty to respect this right in others (see p.31). Locke felt, however, that natural rights were a series of specific rights with corresponding duties to others. For Locke (as for Aquinas) natural rights had a definite content. Firstly, human beings had a right to life. For Locke, this was a form of property right: one owned one's own body. It followed that no one could be born the property of someone else, for instance a slave or a serf. This right to life was inalienable, which meant that it could not be sold to anyone or otherwise disposed of. Secondly, human beings had a right to the products of their own labour. When people worked, they 'mixed their labour' with some raw materials, which thereby became their property. To Locke, it was as if labour enclosed parts of the great common which is nature. Once a person had appropriated part of nature in this way, then other people had a duty not to interfere with it, and the owner had a right to prevent them from trying to do so. But there was a limitation on the natural right to appropriate unoccupied parts of nature; it was unreasonable, Locke held, and contrary to natural right, to appropriate more than one could use, and it would be equally wrong to take so much that there was not enough left for others. However, he regarded the state of nature as basically a state of plenty. (The fact that America was being colonized and that there seemed to be no end to the amount of land which could be taken from the Indians had an important role in Locke's thinking.) Whereas for Hobbes the state of nature was a state of war, for Locke it was a state of basic peace. According to Locke, if institutions like the state and the legal system were necessary, this was because a few stupid or evil people insisted on exceeding their natural rights and taking the life and property of others. In order to have an efficient defence against such people, it was necessary for peace-loving respecters of property to organize a state apparatus which would legislate in accordance with natural rights, and enforce this legislation. The power of the state, therefore, was based on a contract between the members of

society who transferred their natural right to punish viol-
ations of natural rights to authorities specially created for
this purpose. These authorities were to be elected for a
fixed term by a simple majority vote, and everyone participating was expected to agree in advance to accept
whatever the majority might decide. Those who were
elected were themselves parties to the contract, and were
not above the law; they held power by courtesy of the
electors, who were sovereign. In this way, Locke's social
philosophy argued from liberal principles in favour of a
constitutional and democratic government.

What kind of democracy did Locke envisage? According to the rather elastic basic principles of his philosophy,
everyone had an inalienable natural right to life and to
his own body. But with dubious consistency, Locke made
an exception of prisoners taken in a just war, who could, in
his opinion, be legitimately enslaved. Again, Locke held
that in a state of nature, no one had a right to take more
land than he and his family could use: that would be
wasteful. But this ceased to be so as soon as money was
introduced (which Locke thought happened prior to the
formation of the state); for then anyone who produced
more than he could use need not squander it, or leave it to
rot: he could sell it for money, for gold or silver, which
neither moth nor rust would corrupt. It was not contrary
to natural law to possess far more of this than one could
ever use. Locke considered that money also modified a
person's natural right to property. In principle, this was
limited to what one could mix one's own labour with. But
if someone bought another's labour, then, according to
Locke, it became 'his' labour: the turf cut by the servant
and the corn sown and harvested by the day-labourer
belonged to the master because he owned the labour
which had been mixed with them.

Locke also thought that in a state of nature no one had a
right to take so much of anything that there was not
enough left for others. But although this ideal might have
seemed feasible in the American colonies, it was hard to

reconcile it with the situation in an old country like England where almost all the land worth cultivating had already been claimed and where there were obviously many people who had no land at all. Locke argued, however, that this was justifiable because the wealth of the nation was so greatly improved by all the labour which had been mixed with the land, that even a landless English day-labourer had better food, clothing, and lodging than the king of a large, fertile but uncultivated country.

According to Locke, those who did not already possess some land or who were not skilful, diligent and parsimonious enough to be able to buy some, would have to sell their labour power to those who had land. This meant selling their right to the products of their own labour, which implied becoming the tools of other people and hence losing their rights as citizens. After all, if the purpose of the state was to safeguard property rights, then those without property were not entitled to have any influence on the government. Those who did not make use of their natural right to property renounced their right to a say in government, just like criminals. In the same way, women and children could not have the vote because of their lack of independence.

Locke's political conclusions correspond very closely to arrangements in England after the Glorious Revolution of 1688. The population was about 5,500,000, of whom 1,300,000 were adult males, and out of these fewer than 250,000 had a vote. In most places elections were conducted by a show of hands in the presence of the candidates, and the candidates usually had ways of favouring those who voted for them and making life difficult for the rest. It is not surprising that the new landowning-merchant class was solidly in power in parliament. It should not be forgotten, however, that in spite of its limitations, this was the widest franchise in any country at that time.

It is a basic principle of liberalism that the state is a servant of the people. But this means different things, depending on who is taken to be included amongst 'the people'. In some contexts Locke seems to have intended it to include the entire adult population, but in others it is clear that he was referring only to adult male holders of property who did not work for others. And this ambiguity was not an innocent or accidental one: it allowed the interest of a relatively small group of men to be presented as that of the whole population. This applied not only to foreign, military and fiscal policies but also to internal ones, where the main service the state was expected to perform was to protect the people and its property against the propertyless nine-tenths of the population – who were not really part of the 'people' after all. This was the political system which Locke's liberalism was used to legitimate.

## Hume's attack on natural rights

In his account of human understanding in general, Locke advocated the principle that true knowledge must be initially based on sense experience; that is, on what is actually seen, heard, felt, and so on. But he did not apply this principle very rigorously. In his social philosophy, in particular, he took it for granted that human beings possess a number of natural and God-given rights and that reason rather than sense experience can discover what these are. The Scottish philosopher, David Hume (*A Treatise of Human Nature,* 1738), applied the principle that sensation is the basis of all knowledge far more systematically than Locke, carrying it to the conclusion that no universally valid knowledge was possible at all, since it would presuppose sense experience of infinitely many instances, which is impossible. Locke had claimed that people have a natural right to the fruits of their own labour, but for Hume this was an empty claim: there was nothing in sense experience corresponding to such rights, so no one could possibly know if they existed. Therefore no philosophy of society could be based on the concept of natural rights. There would be no rights at all in a state of nature, and even if there were, it would be impossible to find out what they were.

For Hume, therefore, the only possible starting point for a philosophy of society was the feelings which people actually have, and the agreements or conventions they actually enter into. He regarded the idea that society was based on a social contract as a useless fiction. In his eyes social institutions had been formed gradually out of enlightened self-interest. They originated in the attraction between the sexes and the need to care for children, which Hume saw in much more positive terms than Hobbes had done. Hume believed that people had a natural liking for the company of others and a natural tendency to help their friends and family, and this, he thought, was the foundation of all social relations. Originally, spontaneous formation of groups of family and friends would have given everyone some experience of the advantages of mutual help, security and trust, and have accustomed people to co-operation (and to a strong sense of the disadvantages of having things they needed taken away from them). Then, as more and more people began to see the advantage of leaving the possessions of others alone, provided others did the same, they began to develop artificial measures to safeguard them. But, as Hume saw it, this did not depend on anything like an explicit contract or promise. It depended, rather, on a tacit convention binding a small circle of people personally known to each other which gradually extended as outsiders became aware of its advantages to all concerned. Ideas of justice and injustice, according to Hume, grew out of such tacit conventions, and were thus neither natural nor dependent on an explicit social contract involving a promise. The same applied to the idea of property, which, as he saw it, was a label for those goods whose constant possession is established by convention. Similarly the habit of honouring promises began as a tacit convention. Gradually, however, as the institution of property became stronger, people began to feel a need for formal procedures to establish who owned exactly what;

and to answer this need, they decided to pay people to specialize in the administration and execution of justice. These people, kings and civil magistrates, were therefore to have the general interest as their private interest.

In rejecting the concept of natural rights, and emphasizing habit and time-honoured, slowly developing conventions, Hume was to some extent attacking a central idea of early liberalism – the idea of thoroughgoing social change guided by the light of reason. But in basing his social philosophy on feelings of pleasure and on the utility of social institutions, he was also foreshadowing a more vigorous, utilitarian form of liberalism.

## The impact of Locke's philosophy in North America and France

Locke's most important work on the philosophy of society (*The Two Treatises of Government*) was written just before the English Revolution of 1688, and it involved a strong attack on absolutist government. Throughout the eighteenth century, it was widely used as a philosophical validation for the political arrangements which existed in England. Outside England, however, the philosophy of Locke was used to justify revolution.

In the English colonies of North America production was based on the individual private-property rights of the farmers, most of whom worked their land themselves or together with a few hired hands. This constituted a more advanced form of capitalism than in England because the farmer did not have to pay a nobleman for the right to cultivate the land, and there was no difference between legal ownership and right of use. In some southern parts of North America the owners of farms and plantations used slaves brought in from Africa. This meant that instead of buying someone's labour for a fixed period, they actually bought workers, who were thus treated in the same way as cattle, totally dependent and with no rights.

The landowners and merchants of the colonies were

repressed, not by a local absolutist king and nobility, but by the English bourgeoisie, who tried to ensure that the territory could be no more than a supplier of raw materials and taxes, and an importer of manufactured goods. In Locke's work the American bourgeoisie found a social philosophy to justify their demand for independence from a state power over which they had no influence. The constitution which was drawn up for the United States of America after the revolution of 1778 owes much to the philosophy of Locke.

In the early decades of absolutism in France (especially 1624-48), the French bourgeoisie had derived considerable advantage from its partial alliance with the king. An efficient mercantilist foreign policy had enabled French merchants to amass large fortunes. A number of public offices had been made available to non-nobles, and members of the bourgeoisie had achieved important positions in government. But around 1700 a number of reversals in foreign affairs had adverse effects on the French bourgeoisie. The nobility began a counter-offensive, and as a result more and more public offices were taken over by noblemen. Thus, France never saw the alliance and merging of interests between the upper levels of the bourgeoisie and sectors of the nobility which was characteristic of England. From about 1725 to about 1780, the wealth of certain sectors of the French bourgeoisie increased enormously, but this was not accompanied by any increase in political influence.

In most matters the French bourgeoisie saw England as a model which France ought to emulate. They saw Newton's physics and the social philosophy of Locke as brilliant expressions of the rational approach from which all progress would have to come. Progress, they thought, depended on a process of enlightenment which involved strengthening people's natural ability to think for themselves, and which, they thought, would overcome the prejudices propagated by traditional authorities like the church and the nobility. This sort of free-thinking was

enthusiastically pursued in the literary *salons* of Paris
where the hope was fostered that an absolute monarch
would introduce enlightened, rational reforms to allow the
bourgeoisie greater political freedom and influence. The
condition of the peasants, who were mostly small tenants
paying rent to absentee landowners, was of little concern
to the bourgeoisie.

## The social philosophy of Rousseau

The smaller artisans and merchants of France, both in
Paris and in the provinces, saw things differently.
In many places, the restrictive practices of the old guilds
and corporations had been broken up. This opened up
new opportunities, but at the same time it made the petty
bourgeoisie extremely vulnerable to competition from the
larger merchants. Most small shopkeepers and artisans
lacked the education and farsightedness to adapt to the
new conditions, even if they had the financial strength to
do so. For many of them freedom was a catastrophy. But
the old system could not compete with the new economic
powers, and so the petty bourgeoisie had no voice in the
decisions which were devastating their lives. As small
proprietors they believed in private property, but they also
felt very bitter towards the rich and powerful and longed
for a return to the secure, regulated world of the past.

The social philosophy of Jean-Jacques Rousseau (*The
Social Contract; Emile;* 1762) can be seen as an articulation
of an intense, if diffuse, protest against these conditions.
Like most of the philosophers of 'the Enlightenment', he
thought that human beings were good by nature. But he
did not think that this natural goodness could be attained
by replacing traditional prejudice with reason. On the
contrary, he believed that enlightenment and the cult of
rationality removed people even further from simple natural virtues like modesty, friendliness and helpfulness. He
pointed out how repression and exploitation had only
been increased with enlightenment and so-called liber-

ation. He regarded the sophisticated *salon* culture of Paris as decadent and morally corrupting. Against the artificiality and pomp of contemporary civilization, he set the ideal of nature. But when he called for a return to nature, Rousseau did not mean a primitive life in the forests, but a life of equality and real liberty in a simple community. He thought of such a society as deriving from a social contract, but unlike Hobbes or Locke he did not think that the contract limited anyone's freedom; rather it created a higher form of freedom. For both Hobbes and Locke, the parties to the social contract gave up part of their freedom to someone else in return for security of life and property. Thus, as Rousseau saw it, they supported political systems which were opposed to freedom. Under absolutism, the people were never free, and in a parliamentary democracy the people were free only at elections, once every four or five years. Rousseau, however, considered that the purpose of legislation should not limit the freedom of the individual, but rather enlarge it. For this reason, sovereignty had to be with the people, and it had to be with them all the time. In a state of nature people would have unlimited freedom to do as they liked, but in reality this freedom would always be severely limited by the interference of others. In a free community, according to Rousseau, the individual would gain a new freedom, the freedom of a citizen, and this freedom could only be limited by the 'general will'. The general will is the will of the community expressing the general interest of the community; and because the individual will is contained in the general will, it cannot really be limited by it – your own will cannot limit your freedom. Thus the kind of legislation which Rousseau envisaged would, he thought, be a direct expression of the will of the people. It would not limit the freedom of the people, but only remind citizens of what they really wanted.

In Rousseau's philosophy the general will is supposed to crystallize as the will of the community as a unified whole, and not just as the sum of individual wills. It should not be conceived of as the outcome of an election or an opinion survey but rather as complete agreement which can be reached through an open, informal discussion in a small group with a shared task. A small village or a corporation of artisans might perhaps reach agreement in this way but it is not at all clear how Rousseau thought this could be done in larger or more complex social units.

The equality which Rousseau advocated did not include the equality of the sexes. As part of his attack on the stilted and tawdry culture of his time he suggested schemes for the free and natural education of children, but what he saw as natural for little boys greatly differed from what he saw as natural for little girls. Girls should be taught how to please men and how to make them love and esteem them, how to be useful to men and to make their lives easy and agreeable. According to Rousseau these were the natural duties of women, and girls should be taught to exercise them from their infancy.

Rousseau went much further than Locke in arguing for equality, not only for property-owners but for the whole male population; and for freedom, not just for the rich and enlightened but also for the poor and ignorant. He showed that the bourgeois call for freedom, as expressed in Locke's social philosophy, was like a demand for freedom for foxes and chickens in a chicken run. But Rousseau offered no real alternative, and his admiration for his native Geneva shows clearly that he regarded it as quite normal and natural that all but a minority of adult males were excluded from political influence. He may have wished for a society where everyone could own some means of production and subsistence but not enough to dominate anyone else. But he made no suggestion as to how such a state of affairs might be instituted or maintained.

## The French Revolution

A series of economic difficulties in the 1780s and a bad harvest followed by a hard winter in 1788 caused widespread distress and discontent in France. At the same time the national debt had risen to what was regarded as a catastrophic level. The nobility tried to take advantage of this situation by demanding greater privileges in exchange for increased taxation. In 1789 this forced the king to summon the old feudal assembly, the Estates General, for the first time since 1614. This assembly was divided into representatives of the nobility, the church and the 'third estate' (this section was dominated by the upper levels of the bourgeoisie and included a large number of lawyers). The third estate gradually gave up hope of an alliance with the king and, by appealing to the aggrieved petty bourgeoisie at crucial moments, they managed to take power. An event of great symbolic value was the storming of the Bastille by a Parisian crowd on 14 July 1789, the Bastille being an old royal fortress and prison which had come to symbolize the arbitrary and cruel rule of the old regime. Land reforms were initiated and work was begun on a new constitution.

In 1793 the king was executed for conspiracy (with other European monarchs) against the French people and its revolution. From then on, France was at war with most of Europe, and its new armies – organized on the principle of a career open to talent and not reserved for the nobility – went from victory to victory. Internally, the government was being increasingly dominated by the most radical and least compromising groups who were responsible for 'the great terror', a purge of the so-called enemies of the revolution, which included many of the original revolutionaries. However, these groups, too, faced insuperable economic problems, and were increasingly dependent on the army, which took power in 1799 under the leadership of Napoleon Bonaparte. The next few years saw a number of wars of conquest which shook the absolutist powers of Europe; but they also witnessed a long series of internal reforms in legislation, administration, education and so on – measures which were to be emulated all over Europe during the nineteenth century and which produced an unprecedented centralization and efficiency in government. The overambitious foreign policy of Napoleon eventually led to defeat and, at the Congress of Vienna in 1815, Europe was reconstructed and absolutist monarchies reinstated in most countries.

## The impact of the French Revolution in England

The French Revolution served as an inspiration for repressed bourgeoisies all over Europe and had adherents amongst the English petty bourgeoisie and artisanry who wanted an extension of the narrow franchise. However, large sections of the bourgeoisie saw the revolution as a terrible warning, a proof that liberalism could be taken too far. The execution of the royal family, the guillotine, and the terror were seen as the unavoidable results of extreme liberalism. Even before the terror, Edmund Burke, an Anglo-Irish member of Parliament, had launched an attack on liberalism (*Reflections on the Revolution in France*, 1790) which is widely regarded as one of the precursors of modern conservative thought.

Burke's conservatism was not based on a refusal to countenance any change at all; he did not wish to preserve everything in the English society of 1790. His conservatism was based, rather, on arguments in favour of certain features of the hierarchical feudal communities which he thought, correctly, were being destroyed. Burke's conservatism takes up some of the themes of Hume's criticism of the liberalism of Locke. Burke thought that the cause of the French Revolution was liberalism, which encouraged individuals to trust their own reason more than tradition. But for Burke, tradition was not a sediment of irrational prejudices, but contained the results of the reason of past generations – results which one ignored at one's peril. Liberalism, by substituting economic relations for traditional communal bonds, neglected such values as solidarity, love, affection and a sense of community. Magnanimity, responsibility, patience, compassion and humility were being ridiculed, and egoism, acquisitiveness and disrespect were being promoted as the new ideals.

To the mechanical view of society of liberalism, Burke counterposed an organic one which emphasized natural communities like the family, and which saw value in traditional, hereditary systems of rank. A nobleman accustomed to power from childhood would wield it with more understanding and compassion than a capitalist upstart who cared only for his profits. A nobleman's family and his close connection with the land would also make him take long-term considerations into account as well as his immediate economic interest.

There is some convergence between Burke and Rousseau in their criticism of the inhuman, cold and cynical aspects of liberalism. But whereas Rousseau's alternative was a vaguely imagined egalitarian community of petty producers, Burke's was a highly hierarchical community held together by 'vertical' personal bonds. Though conservatism became more popular in the years following the Napoleonic wars, and though some farm worker might prefer a conservative nobleman of the old type to the more ruthless modern landowner/capitalist, this did not stop the advance of capitalism and liberalism.

# 5

# Prussian absolutism and the social philosophy of Kant

## Germany 1600-1800

The economic development of Germany suffered a serious setback during the Thirty Years' War (1618-48), and was also hampered by the absence of a German national state. Until 1815 'Germany' was a collective term for about 230 relatively independent units which differed enormously in size and internal organization, and had little in common apart from the German language and a common past within the so-called Holy Roman Empire. The relations of production were basically feudal until after the French Revolution. Prosperous merchants could be found in certain towns, but most of the production was still agricultural and the majority of the peasants were unfree tenants. Their condition was generally better to the west of the Elbe where repression during the fourteenth and fifteenth centuries had been less severe than in the east.

In the east, the Electorate of Brandenburg (or the

Kingdom of Prussia as it became after 1701) gradually emerged as a new political and military force. This was mainly due to a unique agreement between the Elector and the nobility, which gave absolute power to the prince and increased the power of the nobility over the peasants. All peasants were treated as serfs unless proved otherwise, and large-scale demesne agriculture, partly for export, became the nobility's main source of income. At the same time, nearly all noblemen were expected to enter military service. Most of the burden of taxation was borne by the towns and the peasants. On several occasions the town of Königsberg in East Prussia rebelled against this agreement, but the rebellions were easily crushed by the army.

In this highly systematized military/feudal absolutist state, liberalism could flourish, if at all, only in the towns. A pietist form of Protestantism, which emphasized the equality of all before God, was the main consolation of the merchants and artisans. Diligent work and parsimony with the gifts of God formed the basic ethos. It was not just dangerous but pointless to discuss politics. The German bourgeois enlightenment was a timid affair.

## The social philosophy of Kant

The social philosophy of Immanuel Kant, who was a professor of Philosophy at the University of Königsberg, gave a supremely clear and systematic expression to liberalism, but it was set in a philosophical framework which accommodated a complete violation of the principles of liberalism in the actual politics of the state (see his *Groundwork of the Metaphysics of Morals*, 1785; and *Metaphysics of Morals*, 1797-8).

Kant would have agreed with Hume in rejecting the notion of natural rights, but he did not follow Hume to the conclusion that practical issues can be decided only on the basis of feelings, habits and implicit or explicit conventions. For Kant, people could have knowledge of universally valid rights and duties, but this knowledge was derived, not from experience, but from reflection on the nature of the human mind itself. He saw human beings as animals with needs and drives, but they were also rational; animal life was determined by natural laws, but reason was not; human conduct ought to be determined not by laws of nature, but by laws of reason. These laws were laws of freedom, in the sense that to follow them would be to follow nothing but one's own reason. For Kant, the fundamental law of reason was to avoid self-contradiction in one's views and actions; this meant always acting in such a way that the principle of one's action could be made a universal law, so that whatever one did, one should be willing to act in the same way in all similar cases, and to accept others acting in the same way. Thus, if someone were considering lying in order to get out of a difficult situation, he ought, according to Kant, to consider whether he would be willing that the principle of lying whenever you are in a difficult situation should become a universal law. If it did, however, and lying became the rule, then no one could trust anyone and communication would break down completely; it would even be impossible to get out of a difficult situation by lying. This, according to Kant, proved the wrongness of lying. In much the same way, Kant would have argued that since I am a rational being it would be inconsistent of me to allow others to treat me as a mere animal; and that, therefore, to be consistent, I should always respect the freedom of others, never treating them as mere means to my ends.

Thus Kant thought that people could discover within themselves the basis both of their rights and of their duties to others; and that in doing so they would in fact be discovering the rights and duties of all rational beings. If human beings were mere animals, they would have had no duties, and if they were angels without any animal drives, they would have needed none. But in fact they were rational animals for whom the law of reason took the form of the requirement that they act in accordance with reason, rather than giving in to animal temptations.

For Kant, the fundamental law of reason was the categorical imperative. It was categorical in the sense that it was not conditional on anything, and in particular had nothing to do with what might be nice, satisfactory or prudent. Doing one's duty meant acting in accordance with this imperative, but moral virtue involved more than this. In order to be moral, the motive had to be right too: duty had to be done for duty's sake, and not from any ulterior motive. Thus it was a duty not to cheat in trading, but a merchant who carried out this duty only for fear of losing the confidence of his customers would not be acting morally.

Hume's observation that it was impossible to find anything in experience corresponding to the idea of a natural right did not worry Kant; Hume had simply been looking in the wrong place. According to Kant, a person's self-knowledge as a rational being was not based on experience; and it was in this self-knowledge that the foundation for the abstract universal principles of morality, law and politics were to be found.

Ideally, according to Kant, human beings should live in a perfect community of rational beings, a 'kingdom of ends'. In such a community, everyone would have as much freedom of action as would be compatible with everyone else having the same amount. One person's freedom would thus interfere with the freedom of others only to the degree that it was itself blocked by the freedom of others. Freedom would be limited only by freedom. Kant's kingdom of ends – where the freedom of one person does not involve the unfreedom of others – is the most perfect expression of a conflict-and-friction-free egalitarian liberalism. Kant considered this ideal to be universally valid, but he also thought that people had an animal side which constantly got in the way of its realization. In particular it was very far from being realized in the absolute monarchy of Prussia, where serfs had no freedom, and where the bourgeoisie was subject to a feudal nobility. Kant attempted to deal with this problem in his philosophy of law. He divided his subject into private law and public law, and subdivided private law into the law of property, the law of persons, and family law.

The starting point of Kant's reflections on property was that since human beings are rational, they are above nature and have an unlimited right to exploit it. But he did not accept Locke's view that people can make something their own simply by mixing their labour with it. Property rights could not exist unless they were recognized by others. Private property could arise only as a result of an agreed dissolution of common property, so in a state of nature all land would have been held in common. Kant also rejected Locke's view that individuals in a state of nature had a natural right to punish infringements of their property. Such actions would not be punishment so much as revenge. So civil society could not be based, as Locke supposed, on a transfer of the natural right to punish transgressions; nor could it be seen as an attempt to secure a more efficient enforcement of the natural law. Kant said that property as such could not exist except within civil society, and neither could punishment. It was therefore wrong to think that civil society was formed on the basis of a transfer of rights: outside civil society, rights did not exist at all. Kant believed that society increased individual freedom, rather than diminishing it. It created the possibility of regulating human relations in a rational way, instead of leaving them at the mercy of animal nature. He spoke of a social contract as the origin of civil society, but (like Rousseau) only as a reminder that legislation should always be such that it could have been voluntarily agreed by the people.

Kant's account of the law of persons concentrated on the nature of contracts, including the wage contract, which he, like Locke, defined as a purely economic agreement between two parties who were legally free and equal.

In the third and last of his subdivisions of private law, Kant dealt with the relations of husband and wife, parent and child, master and servant, under the general heading of the 'law of persons in the manner of the law of property'. He defined marriage as a contract which gave each party a monopoly in the use of the natural sexual capacity of the other. In the sexual act, according to Kant, each person is treated by the other as a mere animal, and this would be a clear violation of the categorical imperative unless it took place within the framework of a rational contract guaranteeing that the relationship was stable and mutual. This was a contract between free and equal parties, but it was not an ordinary contract. First of all, it was not incompatible with the wife being subject to the rule of the husband, and second, if one of the parties were to desert the other, the contract would not be nullified, since the wronged party would have allowed him or herself to be used as an animal without getting the recompense – in terms of security and mutuality – which he or she was entitled to expect. Consequently the deserter ought to be brought back home like a piece of lost property. Hence, the heading: 'law of persons in the manner of the law of property'.

With children the problem was slightly different. Children, for Kant, were not full persons, so their relation to their parents could not be a matter of contract or of the law of persons. On the other hand, children were not mere things, owned by their parents: they would eventually become mature persons. Still, children were under the rule of their parents, and if a child ran away from home, the parents had a right to have it brought back no less than if it were an escaped cow.

For Kant, the master-servant relation differed from the wage relation in that the servant was a member of the master's household and thus subject to the rule of the master in a more total way than a wage-labourer. A runaway servant, like a spouse or child, could be forced to come back home again.

Thus in order to account for the actual relations between members of a household, Kant had to acknowledge persons being treated as property in a way that was quite incompatible with the ideal of a kingdom of ends.

In his philosophy of public law, Kant advocated a democratic republic as the form of government closest to the ideal; and he argued that hereditary political rank was as anomalous as hereditary professorships would be. However, he ended up by arguing that a constitutional monarchy had considerable advantages, and that where a nobility exists it should be allowed to continue to have political privileges, though the king should not create any new lords.

But how was the ideal of a democratic republic to be achieved? According to Kant, people who had the misfortune to live under a repressive and arbitrary absolute state ought to bear with it. They had a right to complain and protest, but no one had the right of resistance or revolution. That would be a right to take the law into one's own hands, and this would give feelings priority over law, which contradicted the very idea of law. Even the worst tyranny could not justify tyrannicide, and if a people were to put their king on trial and execute him, then it would be murder masquerading under the form of law.

Because of the sharp division within Kant's philosophy between the animal and the rational side of human nature, this moral law constitutes an austere and awe-inspiring, but also impossible, demand on human beings. His emphasis on respect for the moral law and on doing one's duty for its own sake would have been a logical consequence in a kingdom of ends, but when applied to the harsh realities of Prussia it took the form either of an impotent protest against, or of a simple submission to, the law of the crown, which was rather different from the law of freedom. In his social philosophy Kant was constantly torn between his devotion to the authority of reason, in the name of which the French Revolution was begun, and his absolute loyalty as a civil servant to the authority of his earthly majesty, the king. In pure philosophy he extolled the majesty of reason but in practical politics the irrepressibility of animal drives made this either an empty ideal or a legitimation of any law which happened to be in force.

# 6

# The Industrial Revolution and its philosophy

## The Industrial Revolution in England

As we have seen, agricultural production in England was entirely transformed during the eighteenth century by the growth of urban markets. By the end of the century, nearly all the agricultural work was done by wage-labourers, who had to work long and hard to support themselves and their families. These changes, and technical improvements, had enhanced agricultural productivity considerably, but it was still at the mercy of conditions, such as the weather, over which no one had any control. Demand was gradually growing, but transport costs, the seasonal character of production, the perishability of the products and competition all limited the opportunities open to farmers.

In cotton manufacture the position was very different. In the seventeenth century, finished cotton fabrics had been imported from India; but the wool interests had managed to control or prohibit this trade periodically, thus encouraging small manufacturers in northwest England to manufacture cotton goods themselves from imported raw cotton. This was a profitable business and as early as 1750 finished cloth was being shipped to Africa in exchange for slaves who were then exchanged for raw cotton in the West Indies and North America; the cycle was then repeated. From about 1780 this trade was yielding profits of several hundred per cent for owners of cotton gins and, later, weaving machines. The machines were simple and cheap but their use had revolutionary implications. they enabled production to take place indoors, at a steady controlled rhythm, independent of the seasons, the weather, and other uncontrollable factors; moreover, this could be done with a relatively small and unskilled work force. The work was not physically heavy, and women and children could do it; this in turn meant that wages could be kept low since these workers did not have to support an entire family. And if some workers did not like it there were always others ready to take their place. The products were durable and easily transported, and they were so much cheaper to produce than other fabrics that they could be sold easily on any market, even with very high profit margins. Inflation added further to the profitability of investment in the new machinery. The English home market was large, and since English foreign policy and naval power had already given the country an enormous lead in overseas trade, extensive foreign markets were open in Africa, South America and even India–where traditional cotton manufacture was being wiped out by competition and trickery. Cheap raw materials were readily available from the colonies and the southern states of the USA, and the cultivated areas could easily be extended; if labour power was scarce, then more slaves could always be brought in from Africa.

In England itself the enormous fortunes which were made in the early years of the cotton industry were invested in bigger and better machines. At about this time the word 'industry' began to be used to refer to machine production. In earlier forms of production, humans and animals had been the main source of power, and the speed of production had been limited by their capacity. In industry, however, machines were set in motion first by waterpower and later mainly by steam. Artisans became machine tenders; they no longer used the tools, the tools used them. Industrial proprietors controlled many more of the factors of production than landowners could, and industrial workers had a much smaller role in directing their own work than did agricultural labourers. The land-owner might expect a steady income from his property, but the industrial proprietor, reinvesting some of his profits in machinery, could hope for an ever-increasing return on his capital.

From 1830 onwards the production of iron and machin-ery followed textiles in becoming industrialized, and the production of steam engines (invented as early as the 1770s) affected all other industries, and revolutionized transport and mining.

The growth of industry also produced a highly devel-oped division of labour. In simple manufacture, each worker is involved in every stage of the production process; in industry, however, the production process is divided at the points at which machines need 'minding', and workers are stationed at these points with no responsi-bility for any other part of the process. Thus it is almost impossible for industrial workers to have a sense of the meaning of their work in relation to the production of the finished article. Their task is limited to keeping a partic-ular machine in working order.

The new industrial upper class consisted of factory owners, who had often begun as artisans or small-scale manufacturers with some understanding of mechanics. Thus, in the origin of industry, it was neither landowners nor merchants but 'self-made men' who rose to promin-ence; and these different groups of capitalists competed for influence on the policies of the state. By the end of the

1840s the industrial capitalists had secured for themselves very considerable political power.

The counterpart of the successful English manufacturers was the industrial proletariat, the factory workers. They worked long hours on monotonous tasks in noisy factories with dangerous. unguarded machinery. Their living conditions were also miserable. Around the mills, hastily erected unplanned living quarters grew up in hopelessly insanitary conditions. Epidemic diseases became common once again. The houses often belonged to the mill so that if a worker lost his job he was liable to be made homeless too. Inflation eroded wages but the widespread unemployment and the unskilled nature of the jobs meant that the workers were in no position to complain or demand higher wages.

But in some respects the industrial workers were better off than the hundreds of thousands of skilled workers who could get no work. Half a million English weavers lost their living following the full-scale introduction of the steam-powered loom after 1820. Some of them became industrial workers, many emigrated, but most perished through famine, disease and drink. Continental Europe experienced similar disruptions when it was opened to English exports after 1820. Time and again, displaced workers organized local rebellions, sometimes in the form of factory occupations or the destruction of machinery. All these uprisings of skilled workers were quickly crushed, but memories of this kind of industrial action lived on.

The enormous increase of productivity which was achieved by the Industrial Revolution was thus accompanied by a drastic deterioration in the conditions of life for large sections of the population. The sharp division between a class of owners of means of production and a class of workers who owned nothing but their labour power became the most conspicuous social relation, obliterating or transforming all other sorts of social relations and institutions.

## Adam Smith and the social philosophy of 'laissez-faire'

A theoretical account of these newly emerging social relations had been provided by Adam Smith as early as 1776 in the context of a sustained argument against mercantilism *(The Wealth of Nations)*. Mercantilism can be seen as an attempt to apply the principles of domestic, household economics at a national level; it implied that the main goal of state policy should be a positive balance of trade, and a consequent increase of the nation's stocks of gold and silver. But a trade surplus for one nation would necessarily imply a corresponding deficit for others, so international competition would be inevitable. States tried to direct the activities of their citizens in the national interest by means of tolls, duties and direct control of imports and exports together with elaborate and cumbersome systems of monopolies and privileges in the more lucrative trades.

For Smith, however, a positive balance of trade was not an end in itself. National policy should aim at the expansion of the total national product, and this growth should not be seen as something which could be achieved at the expense of other nations. There was no reason why all nations should not be able to increase their wealth. This further implied that political interference with trade or production was against the basic national interest. If individual producers were left to themselves, they would do their best to maximise their production, and so the total national production would increase. According to the optimistic reasoning of Smith, the state should stop interfering in production and then things would look after themselves to the advantage of one and all: *'laissez faire; laissez passer'*. If no attempts were made to plan and organize production on a national or regional level the entirely selfish action of individuals would automatically add up to the socially most beneficial result – an unconscious co-ordination would be achieved, as though it was directed by an invisible hand.

The main way to increase production, according to

Smith, was by developing the division of labour. He observed the enormously increased production which could be achieved by specialization and rational organization within the more advanced manufacturing enterprises of his time, and he argued for the application of the same principles on a national level, so that every producer or manufacturer would specialize in a single kind of product and could rely on the market to ensure that other producers would supply any other necessary goods.

The terms on which products were exchanged were determined, for Smith, by their 'values'. But how was value determined? Smith believed that, in a state of nature where everyone might have been an independent producer and no one employed by anyone else, the value of a particular kind of product would be determined by the average time it took to produce: people would not be prepared to exchange products which they had taken a long time to make, for ones which could be made in a short time. Thus, on average and in the long run, products would tend to be exchanged in accordance with the average time they took to produce; this was Adam Smith's labour theory of value.

However, Smith believed that things were more complicated in civil society (as opposed to the state of nature). Where land was private property, landlords could demand a rent for the use of land, and where stock was accumulated in the hands of private individuals, they could use it to provide work, supplying people with raw materials and wages and making a profit by the sale of their products. Under such modern circumstances the value of a product would be determined not by the labour time required but by the social mechanisms which determine the average levels of wages, rents, and profits. Thus Smith could argue that the growth of industry and of the total national product, the wealth of the nation, would be in the interest of all: landlords, capitalists and workers alike.

A more pessimistic argument, however, was put forward in Thomas Malthus's *An Essay on Population* in 1798, by which time it was more difficult to argue that industry was directly advantageous for the workers. Malthus argued that if there was abundant food, the population would grow in a way which can be represented by an exponential function (or geometric ratio); it would double, say, every ten years. People would breed like rabbits. However, Malthus argued that the supply of food could not be increased by more than a certain amount each year, in accordance with a linear function (or arithmetic ratio). And the population obviously could not continue to grow faster than the food supply. However, if industry, or charity, made the workers more prosperous then more of their children would survive. Then there would be many more people to feed, and, once more, not enough food to go round. Thus industrial prosperity would have the effect of increasing human misery. These, according to Malthus, were the hard facts and no amount of humanism or philanthropy could alter them.

## The utilitarianism of Bentham

If Smith had shown how the structures of industrial capitalism could be interpreted as an improvement on traditional social institutions, the social philosophy of Jeremy Bentham extended this interpretation into the fields of morals and legislation (*Principles of Morals and Legislation*, 1789). Bentham's liberalism accepted Hume's attacks on the state of nature, the social contract, and natural human rights: all such talk, said Bentham, was 'nonsense on stilts'. The starting point of a philosophy of society had to be individuals and their feelings, and the institutions of society and the state could be justified only in so far as they brought pleasure to individuals.

Every human action, Bentham thought, was an attempt to achieve pleasure and avoid pain. People's ideas of good and evil or right and wrong could only be based on feelings of pleasure or pain. So human beings were rather like entrepreneurs dealing with pleasure and pain; just as entrepreneurs try to calculate which investments will bring the best return, so human beings try to calculate which course of action will bring the most pleasure, taking into account such variables as the intensity, duration, probability and propinquity of the pleasure in question. Thus, for Bentham the rationality of the entrepreneur served as a model for human rationality in general. The effect of this, of course, was to make capitalistic rationality appear the most natural thing in the world, and to present industrial capitalists as merely doing with capital and on a large scale what everyone is always doing on a small scale when trying to get pleasure and avoid pain in ordinary life. In Bentham's view there was obviously no place for divine commands, or for natural rights, nor for duties deduced from a reflection on human reason. Actions could be judged only by their consequences; for example, if I could calculate that it would benefit me to lie or to steal, then it would not be wrong for me to do so.

A community, for Bentham, was nothing more than the individuals of which it was composed; and the interest of the community as a whole was simply to maximise the balance of pleasure over pain for its members. Bentham considered that on the whole this interest could not be well served by leaving everything to the free play of individual calculation. It would be better served if there were social institutions which would ensure that people adopting courses of action that would hurt others would suffer artificially inflicted quantities of pain. For instance, the pleasure of stealing should be artificially counterbalanced by pain inflicted on the thief. Such publicly fixed adjustments to the consequences of certain courses of action were, for Bentham, the only justifiable form of punishment. Thus, punishment ought to be seen not as a specific retribution for those guilty of evil, but as a general deterrent from actions that would cause more pain than pleasure overall. In the England of 1780, where the legal system obviously had little to do with utility for increasing the sum total of human happiness, this was a highly subversive approach to the law. There were enormous penalties, for instance, for petty thefts or for disrespect towards noblemen, and these were obviously out of proportion both with the pleasure the criminal could have got from the crime, and with the pain they had caused the victims. Thus the legal system of the time subtracted much more from the happiness in society than it added; and Bentham worked tirelessly to change it. In his youth he believed that the reforms needed could best be brought about by a powerful king, but later he came to believe that the only way of getting government to serve the interests of the governed would be to ensure that sovereignity belonged to the people. In his early works he argued that a limited franchise would both safeguard property and control government; but later he came to think that manhood franchise would be more compatible with the egalitarian basis of his utilitarian principles and that it would present no danger to the free market system, as could be gathered from the example of the USA where propertyless men had long had the vote.

Bentham's social philosophy was a form of utilitarianism: a theory that every action and institution is to be judged purely by its consequences in terms of the pleasure and pain it produces for all concerned. Although it was formulated as an attack on the theories of liberalism based on natural right, it served, like them, as a liberal legitimation of the social institutions of capitalism.

## Liberalism at a turning point

The development of liberalism in the seventeenth and eighteenth centuries corresponded to the changing political situation of the bourgeoisie. At the time of the first English bourgeois Revolution, Hobbes saw human beings as scared animals who could achieve security only by giving absolute power to the state. At the time of the second English Revolution, when the interests of the bourgeoisie were more secure, Locke saw human beings as dignified creatures with innate rights which could be most efficiently defended by giving a limited amount of power to the state. And by the time of the Industrial Revolution, when the strength of the bourgeoisie seemed unlimited, Bentham saw human beings as pleasure-seeking animals who should give no more power to the state than was necessary in order to increase the sum of human pleasure.

What all these three forms of liberalism have in common is the idea that human beings must plan society according to their individual interests, whether in security of life and property, protection of rights, or augmentation of pleasure. At the beginning, liberalism was an attack on the nobility. Hobbes's social philosophy advocated a concentration of power in a supreme ruler who would curb the hereditary power of the nobility and ensure opportunities for social advancement through riches. Locke's conception of natural rights common to all allowed no justification of the hereditary rights of nobles. After the Industrial Revolution, however, the victory over the nobility was complete and there was no point in continuing to condemn their inherited rights. If noble families were to remain powerful, this could only be by adopting bourgeois methods of increasing their economic wealth. Thus, a fusion of the basic economic interests of the nobility and the bourgeoisie had taken place. At the same time, a new force had to be reckoned with: that of the propertyless producers, the industrial working class. In this context, the advocacy of equal rights was not wholly in the interests of the bourgeoisie. The French Revolution had shown how difficult it could be to limit the demand for equality to equality before the law. Bentham's utilitarianism, with its stress on the idea that people are all equal in the great business of life, which is pleasure, served to rule out of consideration any inequalities in initial conditions and opportunities. Bentham's social philosophy presented happiness as a personal achievement and unhappiness as a result of personal shortcomings.

For many sections of the bourgeoisie the utilitarianism

of Bentham was too radical. His attack on traditional moral ideas was too thorough for all but the most cynical capitalists and certain intellectuals. But whether it was popular or not, Bentham's social philosophy sums up and rationalizes important elements in the world view and self-understanding of the new industrial capitalists.

Between 1818, when the last remnants of the guild and corporation systems were abolished, and 1833, when the first rudimentary labour protection laws were enacted, the labour market in England was freer than at any other time. There was also a free market in land, and in nearly all commodities. After 1846, and following a long political struggle, duties on the import of grain were removed, and so foreign trade too was left at the mercy of the forces of a free market. But after this peak, restrictions began to be placed on the operation of the free market, and modifications were introduced into utilitarian theory.

## The social liberalism of John Stuart Mill

Industrialization resulted in social misery on a large scale. This led both to the formation of trade unions for joint action against the mill owners, and to a morally outraged movement amongst the bourgeoisie which brought about political interference in industry, especially concerning the employment of children in factories and mines.

John Stuart Mill's social philosophy (*On Liberty*, 1859; *Representative Government*, 1861) was an attempt to defend utilitarianism by modifying it at various points. The theoretical basis for these modifications was a distinction between higher and lower forms of pleasure. The difference between these could not be registered in the terms which Bentham would have recognized – intensity, duration, and so on. Spiritual pleasures, for example, were higher than bodily ones, and according to Mill, even a mild spiritual pleasure was preferable to an intense bodily one: it was better to be Socrates unsatisfied than a pig satisfied. This distinction enabled Mill to argue that everyone ought to be left free to develop their capacities so that ever-higher forms of pleasure might come within their reach. By the same token, since some forms of pleasure were available only to the educated, the state ought to compel children to go to school, even though they might at first experience more pain than pleasure as a result, and even if parents and employers would prefer them to go to work.

This was a modification of the *'laissez-faire'* version of utilitarianism. For Bentham, the functions of the state should be limited to the enforcement of minimal regulations designed to diminish the frictions and collisions between individuals engaged in their separate quests for happiness. For Mill, the state was obliged to intervene in order to promote the free development of individuals. For Bentham, efficiency was all important: majority rule was preferable because it was the most direct way of securing the greatest happiness of the greatest number. For Mill, the right of every individual to free self-development was more important than short-sighted efficiency, and it had to be protected against encroachment by others, even if they were an overwhelming majority. Freedom of thought, speech and the press had therefore to be preserved at all costs, regardless of whether they contributed to happiness in a particular situation. And if free competition threatened these liberties, the state had to intervene. Mill did not see these liberties as based on natural rights, however: their foundation was the utilitarian principle, subject to Mill's interpretation of happiness and pleasure. Mill went much further than earlier liberal thinkers in arguing for wide democratic participation in government. He was a fervent advocate of equal political rights for women, and also considered that it would one day become necessary to grant the vote to propertyless workers, the majority of the male population; but he argued that this ought to happen gradually, and should not be allowed to outstrip the extension of working-class education. His concern for guarantees of minority rights was heightened by the prospect of mass democracy.

The social philosophy of J.S. Mill is sometimes called social liberalism because it combines a traditional liberal individualism with a concern for the political rights and the personal development and liberty of all. Mill was able to combine these views only because of his belief that, given sufficient education, the working class would appreciate the rationality of the capitalist system. In other words, he had confidence in the strength and persuasiveness of the bourgeoisie; it could, he thought, accommodate democratic political participation by the working class and this would have the advantage of integrating workers into the political system, thus avoiding the danger that they might unite against it.

# 7

# The modernization of Germany and the social philosophy of Hegel

## Germany 1800-48

The rather static political situation in Germany was shattered by the collision with revolutionary France during the Napoleonic wars. The regions to the west of the Rhine came under direct French government and a series of liberal legal and fiscal reforms on the French pattern were carried out, greatly to the benefit of the local bourgeoisie. Full-scale industrial development began in the Ruhr region. In the rest of Germany, and especially in Prussia, defeat by the modernized, meritocratic French army proved the necessity of military and social reforms. The whole Prussian organization of society, with its close ties between the nobility and the army, had been defeated by Napoleon's army.

After 1807, the king and sections of the nobility set about modernizing Prussia, transforming the nobility into a capitalist, landowning class and increasing the economic freedom of the bourgeoisie. Serfdom and labour dues were abolished, a free market in land was instituted and peasants were offered the right to buy their freedom and their own land. The price was extremely high, however, and many peasants had to sell part of their traditional holding in order to buy the rest, or else incur a heavy debt to the lord. The liberation of the peasants thus led, within a few years, to a concentration of land in the hands of the nobility, who were able to introduce improved large-scale methods of cultivation by employing landless, free labourers who had no alternative but to work for the landowner, and who could therefore be forced to work much harder than before.

After the congress of Vienna in 1815 the number of independent German principalities was reduced to thirty-nine, but each was ruled by an absolute monarch. Hence the first stages of the modernization of the various German states were carried out from above, without any formal representation of the bourgeoisie; thus they were always liable to be reversed if the monarch or his noble advisors felt that the development was going too far.

When the Napoleonic blockade against English trade was lifted, Germany was swamped with cheap English goods, especially cottons which virtually destroyed traditional linen production. In 1843 a customs union, or common market, was formed between eighteen German states, dominated by Prussia. This was an important step towards German unification, which was completed in 1871.

The reforms in Prussia of the 1804-14 period affected all levels of education, and included the creation of a new and modern university at Berlin which became a centre of German liberalism and a radical student movement. However, it was also subject to government interference, especially during the decade of reaction after 1819. Georg Wilhelm Friedrich Hegel was a professor at this university from 1817 until his death in 1831.

## The social philosophy of Hegel

Hegel lived through the Industrial Revolution in England and the political Revolution in France, and he went further than any earlier social philosopher in insisting that society and theories of society were essentially historical, forming part of an irreversible development in time. Hegel saw the history of mankind as the actualization of the principle of personal freedom in higher and higher forms. Thus he saw Christianity as progressive in so far as it was a personal religion ignoring the ties of a particular state or social group; and Protestant forms of Christianity went further, emphasizing the exclusively personal relationship between the individual and God. Hegel saw in the private-property rights of capitalism a result of applying this principle of personal freedom to society.

However, Hegel thought it was easy to misunderstand this society of personal freedom. A seemingly obvious point of departure was the Lockean individual, appropriating objects by mixing his labour with them. This approach, according to Hegel, could not lead anywhere; after all, if property rights were based on individual will, there would be no proper way of dealing with infringements of them: there might be revenge, but there could not be punishment. So society could not be understood on the basis of individual appropriation.

Another possible point of departure was the conscience of the individual as portrayed by Kant. This depended on the idea that one should always act in such a way that one would be willing for the principle of one's actions to become a universal law. But for Hegel, this was an equally abstract and one-sided principle, containing no proper way of dealing with evil because, in the final analysis, it left it up to individuals themselves to decide whether an action was good or evil.

The Lockean and Kantian forms of liberalism, according to Hegel, were both incapable of really grasping the modern principle of personal freedom. Their inadequacy was a result of abstracting from the real life of individuals, families and societies. The Lockean individual appropriating objects in nature, or the Kantian individual trying to follow the categorical imperative, were always acting – consciously or not – as members of a family and of a society. It was only on this basis, according to Hegel, that they could claim their freedom; they did not enter these social relations as pre-social free individuals. So the social philosophies of Locke and Kant were false, but not straightforwardly so. Their mistake was that they took abstract aspects of personal freedom for the whole truth about it. Any adequate social philosophy, therefore, would have to preserve the insights of Locke and Kant, rejecting only their one-sidedness.

The family, for Hegel, was based on natural love between the sexes, and it was absurd to view this relation in contractual terms as Hobbes and Kant had done. Of course, the marriage ceremony involved a contract, but, according to Hegel, the effect of marriage was to do away with the legal independence of the two persons, and to create a sphere which was beyond the law. The purpose of marriage was to enable people to achieve a higher form of freedom in which the woman would have a closed, safe domain in which she could develop her instinctive feelings, and where the man could relax after venturing, as it was his nature to do, into the outside world. Children were the embodiments of the love between the parents, and their early development had to take place within the family, though eventually they would have to leave and set up families of their own.

For Hegel, the sphere of life which lay beyond the family was civil society. This consisted of the relations between families, especially in so far as they depended on one another's products. A baker's family, for example, would produce more bread than they could consume themselves, but they could exchange most of their bread for other products through the medium of the market, so that in the end the whole range of their needs would be satisfied. In return other families could specialize in different branches of production and rely on the baker to satisfy their needs for bread, and so on. Hegel considered that the essential nature of civil society had been correctly analysed by political economists like Adam Smith. But unlike Smith, Hegel expected civil society to produce conflicts, and to work to the disadvantage of some social groups. In particular, he thought that if it were left to the free operation of market forces, the result would be a concentration of wealth in a few hands and the creation of a mass of helpless paupers.

Hegel thought that such problems in the free operation of the market called for two countervailing institutions. The first of these was the corporation. This was a form of self organization for the protection of the second of the three estates of civil society. (The first estate consisted of relatively self-sufficient families living off the land; the third, of civil servants who made their living by working for the general good of society. Both these estates were relatively secure. But the second estate, the private estate which comprised town-dwellers living by handicraft, industry and trade, was in a relatively precarious situation.) Corporations were organizations based on particular branches of production and giving otherwise isolated and competing producers the chance of a communal life and a recognized trade. However, even with the development of corporations within the second estate, civil society could not, according to Hegel, be left to regulate itself. Instead, civil society, along with the family, had to be subordinated to a larger, more cohesive unity: that of the state.

The state, as the unity of family and civil society, had to be unified, according to Hegel, by a monarch who would take final responsibility for all decisions. His argument was as follows: unity necessarily involves a decision to end deliberations, and this decision has to be taken by a particular but arbitrarily selected person, the natural method of appointment being the brute fact of birth: the hereditary monarch. Hegel proposed that the monarch should choose a government which would head the executive which carried out his decisions. His decisions, however, would have to be based on consultation both with the executive and with the people. The voice of the people would make itself heard through a parliament with two chambers. The second, or private, estate would be represented through the corporations, which would propose a number of candidates for the lower house, from whom the monarch would pick those he considered most suitable. The first, or landed estate, would be represented through hereditary membership of the upper house. The third or general estate, the civil servants, would not need to be represented in parliament, since they could exert their influence through their work in the preparation of legislation.

Hegel's conception of the state, and his advocacy of a kind of constitutional absolutism advised by parliament, enabled him to indicate how countries like Prussia could be modernized without going through anything like the French Revolution and without risking a dissolution of civil society into unprotected and isolated individuals – something Hegel thought was gradually happening in England.

Hegel's philosophy of society, like that of Hobbes, was based on a vivid anxiety about the potentially disruptive effects of the liberal principles of the new capitalism. Just as Hobbes argued that liberal premises must lead to absolutist conclusions, Hegel argued that there had to be corporations, a nobility, and a monarch in order to control the freedom of civil society: only thus, he thought, could the highest forms of freedom be attained.

Hegel's social philosophy was therefore neither liberal nor conservative. Liberal philosophers had portrayed feudalism as narrow, restrictive and unenlightened, and had criticized it in the name of reason and individual freedom. Conservatives, on the other hand, defended feudal institutions in the name of community and tradition. But for Hegel, the mistake of both parties was to regard reason and tradition, or individuality and community, as irreconcilable opposites. He tried, therefore, to show that reason is always traditional, and that it can never begin completely afresh; or conversely, that every tradition is a phase in the development of reason. Tradition was not sacred, and parts of it might need to be rejected in the light of reason, but reason had its roots in the past, and was constantly developing: none of its phases could claim to represent timeless truth, or eternal natural rights. In this way Hegel claimed to have moved beyond both liberalism and conservatism, abolishing the error of both and preserving the truth of each. His own social philosophy, he thought, signalled a new and higher phase in the development of reason.

Hegel approached the liberal and the conservative portrayals of the relation between individual and society in much the same way, seeking to go beyond both the liberal idea that society is created by and for individuals, and the conservative view of the individual as a creation of society. A compromise between these two positions might be found by speaking of an interaction between individual and society, but Hegel would have none of this. For him, it was absurd to think of individual and society as if they were independent entities which acted on each other. Individualization, for him, was a social process, and at the same time it was nonsensical to speak of a society without individuals. Liberalism was right to envisage the possibility of individuals joining forces and changing society, but equally conservatism was right to see that individuals develop as part of the society they are living in. But each position was wrong in trying to exclude the other. Hegel thought his attempt to overcome the opposition between liberalism and conservatism was the key to the problem of reconciling traditional German society with the liberal ideals of the bourgeois revolutions of England and France. The modernization of Germany should combine the best of the English and French liberal ideals with the best of the German traditions. This would produce a higher form of society, enjoying not only bourgeois liberties, but also communal securities.

Such, at least, were Hegel's intentions. But it is not obvious that his account of the corporations and the state would actually achieve a unity beyond both liberalism and conservatism. The social philosophy of his *Philosophy of Right*, seems, in fact, like an uneasy compromise, setting out confidently from liberal premises, but gradually losing conviction, and hedging liberal principles with powerful checks from above.

# 8

# The rise of the working class and socialism

## The early working-class movement

Until about 1870 England had by far the most highly developed manufacturing industry in the world. More than a third of industrial production took place in England, where textiles, though still important, had been overtaken by engineering, especially the manufacture of steam engines for use in railways, ships, mining and other industries. Railways were built all over the world, mostly by English companies. But the process of industrialization was already well advanced in other countries, especially the USA, France and parts of Germany.

In Europe the process involved the destruction of traditional skills and the collapse of the prosperity of artisans. Many millions of Europeans emigrated, thereby greatly stimulating the industrial and agricultural advance of other countries, especially the USA, and relieving many of the social tensions within Europe.

It is possible to trace the origins of a world economy and of an international division of labour as far back as the sixteenth century; but world trade achieved a new level of importance in the nineteenth century, as railways, steamships and telegraphs began to connect distant parts of the globe, enabling the Industrial Revolution to pose brutal threats to the social relations of so-called 'backward' areas in Africa, Asia and South America.

We have seen how legislation was gradually introduced in England to mollify the worst effects of free competition, and how liberalism was transformed into social liberalism. One motive behind these changes had been the fear that the misery of the working class might lead to revolution; and various sections of the bourgeoisie organized charities to alleviate the poverty and degradation of the working class. However, there were also movements based on the idea that the liberation of the working class could only be brought about by its own activity. The need for organizations based on this principle seemed to be a lesson of the experience of wage struggles and industrial action.

Competition forced employers to keep wages as low as possible, and individual workers had no chance of resisting wage cuts: if they tried, they would simply be dismissed and replaced from amongst the unemployed. Individual workers were always dispensable: they could only defend themselves collectively, by organizing so as to be able to threaten to withdraw their labour power completely. 'One for all and all for one' was the only principle on which the workers could defend themselves; the alternative, 'Everyone for himself and the Devil take the hindmost', would have left them completely at the mercy of their employers. The defence of the interests of the industrial workers had thus to be articulated in terms of ideals quite different from those of the liberal social philosophies made prominent by the bourgeois revolutions.

The clearest practical expression of these new proletarian ideals was the creation first of trade or labour unions and then of national and international federations of unions. These organizations were pioneered in England. The government at first prohibited unions because it saw them as interfering with the free operation of the market, but later, in the early nineteenth century, it had no choice but to legalize them. Politically, the trade unions led the Chartist movement, a campaign for a radical extension of the franchise (which even after the reforms of 1832 excluded most industrial workers, not to mention all women). This movement was defeated in 1848, and for the remainder of the century the English unions were, by and large, engaged in local industrial struggles for better wages and work conditions. This is not to say, however, that the unions were politically unimportant: the threat posed by their existence was clearly the indirect cause of a number of concessions made to the working class in the years following the defeat of Chartism.

On the European continent, where industrial development was on the whole less advanced, small groups of radical industrial workers were active in the revolutions of 1848, most notably in France and Germany, and in this context the working-class movement tended to take a political rather than an economic form.

The political working-class movement developed out of earlier, pre-industrial protest by poor and oppressed peasants and artisans, for example, the radically egalitarian groups active in the French Revolution. These earlier movements were basically directed against rich and powerful individuals or groups. The working-class organizations which were formed after the Industrial Revolution, however, came to see themselves as struggling not against the rich, but against the system which divided the nation into two classes: property owners who need not work, and workers who could not own property. Their political ideal was the abolition of private property in land and machinery, and its replacement by communal ownership and control of all the factors of production and distribution. The realization of this ideal would, it was felt, put

an end to exploitation and result in a classless organization of production where people would work according to
their abilities and be supplied according to their needs.
This socialist or communist doctrine became particularly
influential in France in the first half of the nineteenth
century. Internationally, these ideals became most influential in the form given them by Karl Marx, especially as a
result of his work within the first International Working
Men's Association, from 1864 to 1872.

## Socialism and Karl Marx

The early socialists saw capitalism as an unjust and irrational system which ought to be replaced by communism.
Marx did not disagree, but he criticized the early socialists
for failing to see capitalism in a historical context. Capitalism, according to Marx, had put an end to feudal injust-
ices and irrationalities, but it had replaced them with
others of its own. In doing so, however, it had also created
the possibility of abolishing injustice and irrationality
altogether. Capitalism had developed industry and thereby created the possibility of enormous wealth. It had also
created the industrial working class, which was capable of
establishing communism on the basis of industry. Thus
socialism had been put on the agenda of history not by
intellectuals or idealistic workers, but by capitalism itself.
Marx was by no means the first to criticize capitalism, but
he was the first to do so neither from a feudal point of view
(like Burke) nor from a utopian point of view (like the
early French socialists). He was the first to devise a social
philosophy designed to highlight the possibilities for socialism discernible in actual historical developments.

Marx's approach implied that it was absolutely crucial
to study the forces at work in contemporary society. His
procedure was to combine the insights of German Hegelian philosophy, British economic science (as developed by

Adam Smith and those who followed him, particularly Ricardo), and French socialist ideas and revolutionary experience.

Hegel saw history as the embodiment or actualization of general principles. We have already seen one example of this in his philosophy of the state, where the notion of the sovereignty of the state is first deduced as a timeless necessity, and then presented as acquiring reality in the person of the monarch. Marx saw this as a mystifying and dishonest procedure for legitimizing existing arrangements. Hegel thought he had shown that sovereignty found its realization in the monarch; but all he had really proved was that in certain states the monarch had achieved absolute power. According to Marx, Hegel was correct in seeing social life as an organized whole, developing in a definite direction, though his understanding of this development was inadequate.

For Marx, history was about the development of production rather than the realization of rational principles. In a sense, this meant returning to the ideas of Locke and Smith; but the point of departure for Marx was not the individual labour of a Robinson Crusoe facing nature all on his own. Production was social labour, as determined at a particular point in history. Social labour, for Marx, was the key to social change. It transformed the natural environment, thereby posing ever new problems for producers; producers, accordingly, had constantly to adapt to the new conditions produced by their labour. Agriculture, for instance, was a form of social labour which transformed parts of the earth's surface for human convenience. This made it possible for people to settle in one place instead of living the migrant lives of hunters and shepherds, and this in turn encouraged the development of new skills and customs. But although agriculture solved certain problems, it created others of its own, requiring new tools and techniques and forms of social organization. These led to further changes in the natural environment, setting new tasks for social labour, and so on.

The fundamental distinction in terms of which Marx portrayed these processes was between forces of production and relations of production. The forces of production included the knowledge and skill of the producers, together with their tools and raw materials. Marx thought that there was a natural tendency to strive for an expansion of the forces of production, and that this tendency produced the basic dynamic of all social development. The relations of production, for Marx, were the forms of social organization through which the forces of production were used – the dependencies between producers and non-producers, the system of property rights, and so on. According to Marx, the relations of production depend on the forces of production. If a particular set of relations of production obstructs the expansion of the forces of production, then they have to be altered. But they will not change either gradually or automatically; they have to be remodelled by conscious action.

Marx's approach to historical change can be illustrated by reference to the transition from feudalism to capitalism. For Hegel, this transition was a result of the fact that the principle of free individuals, having revolutionized the sphere of religion and philosophy, had begun to take over social production as well. For Marx, the transition was a result of the expansion of the forces of production through the adoption of new techniques in agriculture and industry. It was in order to accommodate this expansion that feudal tenants were reduced to landless labourers, through the intervention of a new class of modernizing, capitalistic landowners. Marx acknowledged that the liberal principle of free individuality played a part in this process; but for him it was not a cause, so much as part of the consequent self-understanding of the new ruling class.

According to Marx, capitalist relations of production are as exploitative as feudal ones, but liberal ideas of individuality had the effect of concealing this fact. One characteristic of feudal relations of production was the transfer of part of the fruits of the peasants' labour to the lord. For instance a serf might have had to work an average of three days a week on the demesne before he could work on his own land. This was an undisguised form of exploitation. The work of wage-labourers, however, is not divided in the same way. In a sense, they have to work for someone else all the time, but on the other hand they are paid for their work. However, Marx claimed that the wage-labourer is as exploited as the peasant, though in a less obvious way: the wage-labourer has to produce goods which can be sold for more than their cost of production, and this cost, of course, includes the workers' wages; so the workers might spend only half their week working to cover the costs of production (raw materials, machinery and wages), and the other half of their time would be devoted to the capitalists, just as half the peasant's time was devoted to his lord.

This analysis represents what Marx regarded as his main discovery, the secret of the capitalist system. It can be formulated as follows: what the capitalist gets from his wage-labourers is the fruit of a certain number of hours of work; but what he pays for is the workers' labour power (in other words their capacity to come and work for him). He pays, that is, enough to keep his workers fit to work, which is to say, the amount necessary for his workers to purchase what they need in order to survive. It is this difference between the value produced when his workers work for him and the value of the wage he pays, which, after deduction for machinery and materials, provides the capitalist with his profit.

From the point of view of the capitalists the sole purpose of production is profit. High quality and large output interest capitalists only in cases where they can be expected to increase profits. Profit is necessary not only for the private consumption of the capitalists but also, more importantly, for financing the investments which will make future profit possible. And unless a capitalist can ensure his future profits, his days as a capitalist will be numbered. This means that it is important for all capitalists that as many factors as possible of production, distribution and consumption are under capitalist control. This means that there is a tendency for all areas of life to be forced into forms which are favourable to the interests of capital; this applies to living conditions, transport, education, health services, communication, recreation and so on.

Within production itself the main implication of Marx's analysis is that the capitalists have an interest in depressing the wages of the workers, whilst the workers have a basic interest in the abolition of capitalism and a short-term interest in higher wages. This conflict of interests, according to Marx, is a crucial fact about capitalist societies. A class struggle takes place, even if individual capitalists and workers may deplore, ignore or deny it.

Smith had recognized a division of society into three classes – landlords, capitalists and workers – but he saw no necessary conflicts of interest between them, and thus no necessity of class struggle. He saw the dynamic of capitalist society as resulting from the increasing division of labour, and he believed that it would lead to a gradual increase in the wealth of capitalist countries, thus benefiting all their inhabitants. According to Marx, however, this growth would be crisis-ridden rather than steady and harmonious.

Put in a very simplified way, Marx's analysis was that it was in the interest of every firm that all other firms should pay their workers high wages, so enabling them to buy more of the commodities produced by the firm in question. But each firm would try to keep its own wage costs down, thus making the workers poorer, and tending to reduce demand and create a crisis of over-production. Firms would then have to cut prices, and some would not be able to survive. This would put workers out of work, which would tend to deepen the crisis by lowering demand even further, though it would also tend to lower the wages which workers were ready to accept (unemployment being a greater threat). The firms which survived – those with the best productivity – would then be able to increase their profit and invest in new activities and employ more workers and thereby stimulate demand again. The crisis would then be over and a period of expansion would begin, though it too would eventually lead to a new crisis of over-production.

## Marx on the state

Hegel would have agreed with Marx that civil society would be threatened with crisis if left to itself. But Hegel thought that the state could and should uphold general national interests against the particular interests competing within civil society, and thus avert the risk to the system.

In his earliest writings Marx had criticized this view of the state in the name of radical democracy. Government, he felt, should be by and for the people, and should not be left to a bureaucracy elevated above society. But he soon abandoned this position, and began to argue that the state and its bureaucracy were not really above society at all. In a class society, he thought, the state was a tool of the ruling class, even though it might seem to be a sort of neutral umpire between conflicting interests. In a capitalist society, then, the state was an instrument of the capitalist class. It might not serve the demands articulated by capitalist organizations, and it could not serve all capitalist interests equally; it might even sacrifice some of them or make general concessions to the working class; but as long as the society was capitalist the state would strive to uphold capitalist relations of production, and, in particular, private property rights in the means of production.

However, the state could not prevent crises of capitalist production. According to Marx, these recurrent crises would lead, on the one hand, to an increasing concentration of control over capital, and on the other, to an increase in the power of working-class organizations. In some future crisis, the situation would become so desperate that the working class would be able to serve its basic interest by destroying the capitalist state itself. In most countries, according to Marx, this was unlikely to be a peaceful transformation, since the ruling class could hardly be expected to give up its position voluntarily. But sooner or later a revolution would succeed and a classless society would result; surplus production would benefit the whole of society, and firms would co-operate, rather than compete, their tasks being determined according to a plan of the whole of social production. At first this task would necessitate the creation of a socialist state apparatus but gradually this would wither away, since a socialist society without class conflicts would have no need for oppressive state machinery.

Marx was never very specific about what a communist society would be like. But the idea of such a society was not a vague utopian ideal loosely attached to his historical analysis of capitalism. In all of his work Marx implicitly used the idea of conscious, direct and democratic planning of social production in order to show up the complications and perversions of capitalist society.

Most earlier social philosophers saw the state as the most important human institution and argued that it is somehow grounded in divine ordinance or eternal human nature. For Marx, the task of social philosophy was not that of justifying a particular type of state; it was rather to criticize the existing, oppressive capitalist relations of production and to expose the class character of liberal social philosophies.

Within the International a power struggle took place between, on the one hand, groups which, following Marx, insisted that the fight against capitalist exploitation was the most important task for the labour movement and that preparing and organizing in order to take over state power was crucial for this fight and, on the other hand, anarchist groups which insisted that all forms of oppression should be resisted and that capitalism should be replaced immediately by a stateless society. The anarchists were officially expelled from the International in 1872 but not long after that the whole association was dissolved owing to lack of support.

## Reformist and revolutionary socialism before 1914

By 1870, England's industrial power had been outstripped by that of the USA, and was about to be overtaken by that of Germany. From about 1873 the world entered a long and serious economic crisis. The boom of the 1850s and 60s had been based to a large extent on the construction of railways all over the world. The rapid expansion of this sector slowed down, competition in the traditional industrial sectors intensified, and the rate of profit fell. Agriculture in Europe was also hit, because railways and steamships made cheap, high quality grain from America and Russia available in large quantities.

Many firms had to close, and those which remained were often left with a virtual monopoly in certain commodities. Where this did not happen a widespread formation of trusts and cartels frequently had the same effect. This meant a great concentration of the decisive influence over industry (although, formally, it coincided with an extension of legal ownership of industry through the formation of joint-stock companies with large numbers of share-holders).

One sign of the crisis was falling prices. This meant that for those workers who could find employment, real wages did not fall, even though the weakening of the working-class organizations as a result of unemployment resulted in lower money wages and other setbacks. The predicament of the unemployed was catastrophic and there was massive emigration.

Economic growth did not really begin again till about 1896. When it finally came it had to do partly with the purifying effects of the crisis which had killed the 'lame ducks' of industry, and partly with an increasingly aggressive exploitation of the natural resources and cheap labour of the colonies. The rush to secure new colonial possessions in Africa and Asia required state expenditure on armaments, and this in turn was an important stimulant to the economy. The recovery was thus linked with imperialism, nationalism and militarism.

The crisis had made union activity both more necessary and more difficult. A certain radicalization of the traditional pragmatic line of the English trade unions took place during the period, and in Germany both unions and socialist parties grew. The latter were united in the Social-Democratic Party of Germany in 1875. It was outlawed and prosecuted during the 1880s but emerged with great electoral strength when the attempt to outlaw socialism was abandoned. The Second International was formed in 1889 (at a meeting commemorating the French Revolution) and was based on Marxist principles.

Within the International and within the Social-Democratic Party of Germany there was a debate, around the turn of the century, about whether the working-class movement should go on adhering to Marxism. In the German party, Eduard Bernstein and his followers held that Marxism needed to be revised. The new prosperity, they felt, made Marx's vision of a capitalist catastrophe seem less convincing. The poverty of the working-class did not seem to be getting worse, and the electoral successes of the Social-Democratic party made it seem possible that the state could be gradually taken over by the party. Thus, many began to prefer reformist rather than revolutionary approaches to socialism. Graduated income tax, they felt, would lead to a more just and equal distribution of wealth, and piecemeal nationalizations of crucial means of production would gradually enable the working class to direct the economy through the state.

The reformist perspective involved a revision of the Marxist view of the state; it came to be seen not as an instrument of oppression, but as a neutral agency which could be run by representatives either of the capitalists or of the workers. This implied that the working class ought to try to expand the influence of the state in all areas of social life, because electoral strength could then be used to achieve real social power.

Many revisionists saw the Hegelian influence on Marxist thought as disastrous, and sought to lead the working-class movement back to a social philosophy based on Kant. Socialism, according to them, should thus be seen as a kingdom of ends, an ideal which socialists should struggle to bring as close to reality as possible. At the same time, commitment to the ideal of socialism should not be allowed to destroy law and order.

Bernstein's revisionism was overwhelmingly voted down, both within the German party and within the International; but in spite of this, revisionism became increasingly influential in the German party, the British Labour Party (founded in 1900) and in most of the other European social-democratic parties. However, many of these parties continued to contain revolutionary socialist elements, quite powerful ones in some cases, especially in Germany and Russia.

# 9

# Social philosophies in the twentieth century

## The Russian Revolution

World-wide industrial competition between the European powers, coupled with their race for the colonies, were among the basic causes of the First World War. Within the social-democratic parties of the Second International, it had been widely believed that solidarity between the workers in different countries and a collective, co-ordinated refusal to fight would prevent any such war. But nationalism proved more powerful than international socialism. When the World War came, the social-democratic parties and the unions supported their own countries; loyalty to national bourgeoisies took precedence over solidarity with the workers of other countries. The conferences of the International were discontinued and, in the belligerent nations, unions voluntarily renounced the right to strike. In most countries there was some dissent from this line; but it was only in the illegal

Russian party that there was a majority which consistently opposed the war.

By European standards Russia was a very backward country. The feudal mode of production had been officially abolished only with the liberation of the serfs in the 1860s. As in other countries, this worked mainly to the economic advantage of the landowners. There had been some rapid industrialization, mainly directed by the absolutist state or by foreign investors. The state also led an ambitious policy of colonization in North-East Asia. The condition of the proletariat was far worse than in the rest of Europe and this in turn meant that the internal market for the products of Russian industry was much smaller than the size of the population might have suggested. There was nothing to compare with the relatively prosperous layer of skilled workers which had formed in West Europe and the USA. Trade-union activity and socialist agitation were prohibited by law and police persecution was severe. Working-class organizations were thus forced to work clandestinely, and many of their leaders were in exile. An attempted revolution in 1905 was crushed. In the years that followed, the split within the Russian Social-Democratic Labour Party between reformists and revolutionaries became wider, and whereas economic growth and concessions from the bourgeoisie had encouraged reformism in Western Europe and the USA, no similar development took place in Russia.

The majority, or 'Bolshevik', wing of the Russian Social-Democracy was led by Lenin. As a political refugee in Western Europe he had seen how trade unions and socialist parties could be accommodated within capitalism, where workers might prefer short-term, economic advantages to long-term, political victory. They would be more likely to support the reformist demand for 'a fair day's wage for a fair day's work' rather than fighting for the abolition of wage-labour as such. Lenin concluded that only a small, well-organized and tightly disciplined party of resolute professional revolutionaries would be able to stick to the long-term goal of proletarian political power, without being tempted by the distractions of reformism. Such a party would be organized on a basis of democratic centralism, that is on the principle that after free and open discussion within the party, decisions would be taken by means of a ballot, the result of which would be adhered to without demur by all party members, including those who had voted against it. All disagreements would be kept within the party, which would thus always be outwardly united and determined.

This conception of the party was discussed within the International and criticized not only by reformists but also by revolutionaries like Rosa Luxemburg. She and her followers within the German Social-Democratic party were afraid of the party becoming an élite, and saw dangers in over-strict party discipline. They considered decentralized, spontaneous, 'grassroot' movements more important than a centralized party. Both groups worked for a classless society where armies, prisons and police would be superfluous because there would be no ruling class trying to protect its privileges and power. Lenin, following Marx, thought that it would be necessary temporarily to replace bourgeois states (dictatorships of the bourgeois minority) with a workers' state, a dictatorship of the proletarian majority, which would ruthlessly stamp out counter-revolutionary movements and exterminate the remnants of bourgeois domination at all levels. On this point, too, the left wing of the German Social-Democratic party disagreed with Lenin. They believed that a classless society should be democratic and decentralized; and they argued that the advent of such a society would be delayed indefinitely, or even prevented, if one form of state repression was simply replaced by another, and if the democratic end was used to justify undemocratic means.

The war with Germany brought Russia to the verge of collapse. A mutiny in the army and the navy and an uprising of peasants and workers in February 1917 brought a coalition of liberal and reformist socialists to power, but disagreement about whether to continue the war, and hesitation in the face of the enormous social problems of the country, led to growing chaos. In this situation the Bolshevik fraction of the Social-Democratic party was by far the most efficient political organization and in October 1917 they took power after a new uprising of soldiers, peasants and workers – now organized in local committees known as 'soviets'. The country became a federal soviet republic and later the Union of Soviet Socialist Republics, and the Bolshevik faction of the Social-Democratic Party became the Communist Party of the Soviet Union. A peace treaty with Germany was concluded and the new republic was successfully defended by its 'red' army against the 'white' (counter-revolutionary) armies which attacked on several fronts with substantial support from the Western powers. The last of the white armies was defeated by late 1920. Economic collapse was avoided but only at the cost of great sacrifices and through the application of brutally harsh methods. Then, from 1920 onwards the transformation of a vast and overwhelmingly rural country into a unified, industrial society began.

The first socialist revolution had occurred, but in a country with an underdeveloped agrarian economy, and not – as Marx's theory seemed to predict – one where the forces of production were highly developed. According to Lenin, this was because capitalism had become an international, rather than a national, mode of production; capitalist crises were now on an international scale, and socialist revolutions were therefore bound to be international too. But they would break out first where capitalism was weakest and where its state apparatus was least efficient.

In the period immediately after the Russian Revolution, the belief of the Soviet Communist Party was that there would soon be a socialist revolution in Western Europe and that the more advanced countries would then support the construction of the Soviet Republic with their technology and investments. But this revolution did not come, although there was an abortive attempt in Germany at the end of the war in 1918. Thus the Soviet Union became an isolated power in a hostile world, and had to rely on its own resources. Its basic priority became the creation of socialism in one country, rather than to await an international revolution. After a brief period of struggle following Lenin's death in 1924, Stalin emerged as leader of the party and thus of the country. He resolutely followed the line of 'socialism in one country' despite initial opposition.

One of the first measures of the Russian Revolution was the nationalization of land: large estates were divided up and the rights to use and cultivate them handed over to peasants and land-labourers. For most of the 1920s the state adopted a policy of not intervening directly in decisions about agricultural production and distribution. Peasants were left to grow and sell their products individually and however they pleased. This system led to a rapid regeneration of agriculture but it also produced a class division between prosperous peasants and those employed by them. From 1928 a centralized, general system of economic planning based on five-year periods was instituted. At the same time a state programme of forced collectivization of agriculture was begun, and 26,000,000 individual peasant holdings were merged to form 200,000 collective or co-operative farms. In spite of enormous problems and numerous mistakes there was rapid progress in the mechanization of agriculture, the construction of power plants and the expansion of heavy industry.

This growth was consciously seen as preparation for the country's survival in case of war with one or more of the Western powers. In this respect it proved to be successful. But politically the dictatorship of the proletariat did not give way to increasingly democratic social planning; it led rather to the dictatorship of a smaller and smaller group of party officials. The element of open and free discussion amongst the rank and file of the party was drastically reduced and democratic centralism was in effect made into a means for the dissemination and enforcement of decisions made by a very narrow clique. Opposition was not tolerated either within the party or outside it: it was crushed by vast and brutal purges.

The creation of the Soviet Union meant that, for the first time, the idea of socialism was used to justify an existing social system rather than as a basis for a more or less determinate critique of capitalism. This completely transformed the context of all debates about socialism. In the West the identification of socialism with Soviet life meant that it was easy for liberals to launch sweeping attacks on socialism on the basis of more or less accurate and comprehensive accounts of harsh Soviet realities. The splits between reformists and revolutionaries, and between Leninist revolutionaries and left socialists deepened. After the First World War the Second International became the organization of explicitly reformist social-democratic and labour parties, and these began to play an important part in the government of most Western European countries. The Third International, or Comintern, was formed by the factions which had broken away from the social-democratic parties, and which supported the Soviet Union. For the Third International, the events of the revolution had demonstrated the correctness of Lenin's belief in a disciplined and centralized party: it was, they argued, the only organization capable of carrying through and consolidating a revolution. They also claimed that no road to socialism in Europe existed which did not involve an alliance with the first socialist country. Consequently each national communist party had to support Soviet foreign policy, defend the Soviet Union against bourgeois criticism, and suppress open discussion of these issues within the party.

But there were other parties and individuals on the revolutionary left who – for various reasons – regarded the Soviet Union as a traitor to socialism. Their work produced some theoretically sophisticated discussions, especially in Germany and in emigré circles in the USA;

but none of these had any real base in, or contact with, working-class movements or organizations.

## Europe between the World Wars

The First World War brought an important extension of democratic participation as male parliaments and male electorates acceded to women's demand for the vote and for equal political rights. In a few countries this had happened before the war (New Zealand 1903; Norway 1905) but it was the involvement of women in war-work on the home front which gave the decisive impetus for the campaign for women's rights in most of Western Europe and in the USA. Russian women achieved equal political rights through the revolution. (In a few European countries, however, such as Belgium and Switzerland, women did not get the vote till after the Second World War. Property and literacy qualifications for inclusion in the electorate were also quite common until after the Second World War, for instance in the USA where they were mainly used to deny political rights to blacks.)

From about 1920 onwards capitalist economies were again dominated by a tendency towards recession culminating in the great crash on the New York stock exchange in 1929. Unemployment was high and strikes and lock-outs were common. Many people, especially amongst the petty bourgeoisie – suffering badly from the crisis – felt threatened by the revolutionary socialist perspectives which had revived as a result of the crisis. To these groups, it appeared that the crisis would be solved only if social unrest and socialist agitation were suppressed and if the anarchic freedom of big capitalists was limited. They therefore supported a political programme of 'law and order', prohibiting strikes and lock-outs and settling disputes on the labour market by legislation, without regard to negotiations between employers and workers. They wanted wages to be fixed by law at a level sufficient to assure most firms of at least a moderate profit. This systematic, legally sanctioned state direction of the labour market in a capitalist economy is an essential element of all forms of fascism. In effect it abolishes the right to negotiate and strike and is usually accompanied by restrictions of civil rights such as the freedom of assembly, of association, of speech and of the press.

There were fascist groups all over Western Europe in the 1920s and 30s, and in Italy, Portugal, Germany and Spain fascist parties got into power. Originally the word 'fascism' was applied to the ideas of the Italian Fascist party under Mussolini, which governed Italy from 1922 to 1943. Attempts to justify fascism usually involve an appeal to the nation, whose interests are taken to be overriding, and thus to legitimate the suppression of class interests. Italian fascism involved a systematic cult of the state, with Mussolini referring back to the legacy of the Roman Empire and exploiting a widespread fear of communism and revolution.

The German form of fascism, Nazism, tried to support Hitler's rule by means of racist ideas about the supremacy of the Aryan race and the historical mission of the German people, and by harping on the supposed injustice of the peace treaty which concluded the first World War. Jews, communists, homosexuals and others were made into scapegoats, and the rest of the people united in persecuting them in a national chauvinist, irrational spirit based on an anti-intellectual cult of blood and soil. Mass support for the Nazis came from the petty bourgeoisie, but from its early years the party also received financial backing from big industrial interests, attracted by the promise of crushing the trade unions, as well as the prospect of growth in the armaments industry.

Fascism is not a specifically German or Italian phenomenon. It is a way of running any capitalist economy, a way which is bound to be tempting to strong capitalist interests when a crisis reaches such great proportions that the social unrest accompanying it seems to threaten private property in the means of production.

## Liberalism and state intervention after 1945

The crisis in the capitalist economy continued till after the Second World War. The destruction of productive capacity during the war made the remaining industries more profitable and the emergence of the USA as the absolutely dominant power, investing capital around the world, laid the basis for rapid economic growth in the non-communist world.

At the same time, the role of the state in non-communist countries became far more important. In terms of personnel and expenditure the size of the state apparatus grew enormously. In countries where reformist social democratic parties were in power this was in accordance with the official line of the Second International, and for years public debate about socialism was conducted in terms of arguments for or against increases in public expenditure.

But, in fact, the growth of state power has also been furthered by liberal parties and conservative parties as well as socialist ones. This has meant, for them, a break with the traditional liberal doctrine - the idea of minimum interference by the state. The theoretical background of this departure is mainly to be found in the works of the English economist John Maynard Keynes (in particular *The General Theory of Employment, Interest and Money*, 1936). According to him, dangerous tendencies in capitalist economies could be prevented if the state would expand public expenditure in non-productive sectors of the economy such as transport, communication, education and health. This policy would not lead to overproduction, but it would increase demand by keeping unemployment down. Such expenditure would also be beneficial in other ways: improved transport and communication would help trade, and a literate and healthy work force would be more productive. This line of argument might also be used in justifying nationalization or state support of unprofitable enterprises (coal, gas and electricity for example) on which the rest of industry depends. At the same time, Keynesian policies could be expected to quell social unrest since payments to the unemployed, social-security schemes, and improved education and health services could be seen as concessions to the interests of the working class or other oppressed groups. These Keynesian policies made room for substantial agreement between reformist socialists and social liberals, and thus led many to argue that political ideologies were dead and that only technical economic questions remained.

During this boom, an unprecedented level of mechanization and automation was achieved both in manufacturing industry and in 'white collar' work; this meant a drastic reduction in the number of skilled trades and a levelling out of the general level of skills needed in various labour processes. This development was accompanied by a further reduction of employment in agriculture, and by a vastly increased participation of women in industry. Within both the public and the private sector there was a dramatic expansion of service industries, while in an international context former colonies carried on as exporters of raw materials and importers of foreign technology, greatly to the advantage of the main capitalist countries in Europe and the USA.

After the defeat of Nazi Germany, Europe was split in two, East and West, roughly along the same line as that which divided areas of successful from unsuccessful feudal repression after the crisis of the fourteenth century. Eastern Europe was occupied by Soviet armies and socialist relations of production were introduced there. In 1949, after a long civil war, there was a successful communist revolution in China. Consequently it began to seem that socialism was advancing rapidly throughout the world, and fear of this led to the Cold War which was at its height in the 1950s. The Western powers sought to isolate the socialist world economically and to fight socialist movements wherever they appeared throughout the rest of the world. In their propaganda, they identified socialism with the harshest and most repressive aspects of the socialist countries. The notoriously undemocratic character of the regimes of Eastern Europe made it virtually impossible to see socialism as a possible extension of democracy in Western Europe. Most democratically minded people, including most social democrats, became anti-socialist and many socialists felt obliged to defend undemocratic uses of power.

Socialist conceptions were virtually excluded from social science and social philosophy as well. Like the Keynesian economic theories which accompanied them, the dominant conception of society and social life in the post-war period originated mainly in pre-war theoretical developments.

In particular, theories about logic and language seemed to provide a foundation for atomistic and individualistic views in almost all theoretical fields. It was thought that 'logical analysis' could be used to sort linguistic expressions into ones which are strictly meaningful and scientifically justifiable and ones which are nonsensical or irrational and not scientifically justifiable. On this basis, questions of value – and especially of what kind of society is preferable – were regarded as expressions of irrational personal feelings with no interpersonal validity. All questions of good and bad, better and worse, right and wrong were seen as similar to questions of whether you would prefer a cheese or a tomato sandwich: they were merely a matter of taste. Scientific or rational thought, so conceived, could have little bearing on the quest for a better society. All it could do was accumulate information about existing societies, and show how various grand phrases in politics – about rights, liberties, or equality – were really only articulations of personal preferences. Morality came to be seen as a personal and private matter rather than as a system of social institutions.

These views received their first sharp formulation in Vienna and other parts of Eastern Europe in the 1920s and 30s. In the semi-feudal and deeply catholic atmosphere of these countries such views constituted a radical and efficient criticism of all kinds of pompous and religious def-

ences of tradition; and they could also be used to attack
fascist conceptions of 'the people', 'the race' or 'the historical task of the nation'. When fascist parties came to power
therefore, this kind of theorizing was abruptly eliminated
in Eastern Europe. But waves of refugees from fascism
spread the ideas to England, Scandinavia and the USA.
During the post-war boom these emigrés formed the back-
bone of a theoretical movement which provided capitalism with a new, cynical self-justification in the period of
the cold war.

   Locke, Kant and J.S. Mill advocated liberalism in the
name of human dignity and equal rights, and in order to
release humanity (or at least part of it) from political,
economic and psychological oppression. The philosophical basis of post-war liberal social philosophy, by contrast, has mainly been the claim that no argument from
objective premises can ever lead to conclusions about how
society ought to be organized. The cynicism of this type of
justification lies in the fact that it refuses to commit itself to
any positive objectives, and in its readiness to agree that it
is itself, like other competing views of society, a merely
irrational personal preference. In a way this might seem to
leave capitalism philosophically undefended, but in a society which is capitalist already, its main effect is to pull the
carpet from under the feet of all critics of existing conditions: it makes it seem that they are merely airing their
own irrational preferences, and that it would be a mistake
to meet them with any argument other than: 'I like one
type of society and you like another, so let us agree to
differ'. This approach tends to reduce any struggle for
socialism to a logical fallacy and to define people who
persist in believing in it as irrational, intolerant fanatics
who are so conceited that they claim to know what is good
for other people.

   Locke, Kant and Mill thought they knew what was
good for people, and they argued for liberalism on that
basis. But in the post-war period, the main defence of
capitalistic societies became the claim that questions

about what is good for people cannot be answered at all, and that the only thing social scientists can do is describe the actual workings of existing social institutions, or construct models of economic circuits; whilst social philosophers could only analyse the language in which people talk about moral, legal and political matters, avoiding any discussion of whether or not existing institutions should be changed.

## The world after 1968

In spite of the application of policies of crisis management, signs of recession in capitalist economies began to emerge in the late 1960s. Then there were a number of sharp increases in the prices of raw materials, the result being the combination of economic stagnation with inflation which characterized capitalist economies throughout the 1970s.

The economic crisis of low profitability, overproduction and growing unemployment has obvious ecological, political and social dimensions. Increases in the price of oil, uranium and other raw materials reflect shortages which suggest there may be natural limits to economic and technological development, whether capitalist or socialist. Pollution and other long-term threats to the continuation of human life can likewise no longer be ignored.

In terms of international politics the crisis in the developed capitalist countries is connected with a shift of power from these old centres to various sectors of the raw material-producing periphery. Multi-national capitalist corporations have secured a high degree of independence from national states, and rapid industrial development has taken place in several traditionally peripheral countries where labour is cheap and financial conditions favourable (e.g. Korea, Taiwan). This has only added to the difficulties of the competing industries in the central capitalist countries. And the near monopolies which some countries have in certain raw materials have added to the problems both for the centres and for the less favoured parts of the periphery. Even the power of the USA has been undermined, both by the defeat in Vietnam and by the weakening of the US dollar. Growing competition from Western Europe, now organized in a common market, may also lead to greater European independence. Economic and political problems within individual countries are increasingly tied up with global developments, which may eventually make the nation state – the political framework of early capitalist development – obsolete.

The first warning of economic crisis coincided with popular movements around the world which put an end to the political apathy of the 1950s and early 60s. Women began once again to organize against sexual oppression – which persisted in all areas of life even after the acquisition of formal equality of political rights. Ethnic minorities protested against continued official and unofficial discrimination. Students protested against hierarchical educational institutions and demanded a say in their own education. At the same time groups dedicated to revolutionary socialism, but for the most part hostile to Soviet communism, began to attract a considerable amount of publicity and support, if very little power. Ecological concerns about the long-term effects of the present forms of industry have also led to widespread popular concern.

None of these movements, however, has had much to do with the working class and its organizations, which are under increasing pressure as a result of the crisis. This pressure has led to a new wave of trade-union militancy and to retaliatory demands for curbs on union power. This raises the question of whether the capitalist system can survive unless the traditions of democratic politics are overthrown by fascist or semi-fascist measures; and of whether capitalism may be changed in a socialist direction, and whether this is to be done by an extension of democratic rights, or by some system of minority rule.

This field of options defines the themes of all modern

thinking about social life. Just as the opposition between feudalism and capitalism was once the inevitable focus of social thought, the opposition between different forms of capitalism and socialism is equally inescapable today. It is an opposition which, both practically and theoretically, divides and structures social practices, and proposals for social change, as well as more abstract conceptualizations including philosophical ones.

The basic difference between the capitalist and the socialist solutions concerns the social division of labour and property rights. Capitalists consider labour power to be a commodity which can be bought and used for the purpose of increasing private appropriation, and they see unemployment as an essential part of the apparatus of economic regulation. Socialists see labour as a human right, which should be divided in a process of conscious social planning, thus abolishing unemployment. Neither of these polar opposites is unified and stable. Around the capitalist pole, there are possibilities both of increasing managerial control of the labour process through automation and 'scientific management', and also of 'job enrichment', worker participation in management, and so on. Similarly, at the level of state politics, governments might use the law and the police to discipline the working class or, alternatively, they could attempt to integrate trade unions into the economy.

Within capitalist societies the different possible capitalist strategies can be countered with different types of socialist response, but around the socialist pole, there is no agreement on such a response, nor on what the content of socialism may turn out to be. In one, minimal, view a socialist firm might be run in much the same way as a capitalist firm, except that the profit would be appropriated by the whole of the community rather than by private owners of capital. At the other end of the spectrum socialism may be taken to entail a complete abolition of all hierarchies of power or remuneration, total integration between the firm and the surrounding community, and the ending of the division between mental and manual labour. And at the political level, socialists may choose between several views of the role of the state under socialism ranging from the model of a highly centralized global or national planning and administration agency, to that of local self organization and a minimal central state.

Round both poles, the capitalist and the socialist, there are different theories about household organization and the relations between the sexes, about ways of caring for children and educating them, and about ways of dealing with sexuality, illness, old age and death.

All these issues have philosophical dimensions to them; first because existing practices and institutions are impregnated with past social philosophies; and second, because discussions of social questions must always involve consideration of the ways in which social problems are posed, and how new developments should be conceived. These problems, however, are ones to which philosophy can contribute only by going beyond supposedly timeless, unhistorical conceptual questions.

In the past, social philosophy has been concerned with issues of right and wrong in the distribution of labour and property. Philosophers have tried to give explicit justifications for organizing social life in particular ways. Nearly all of them have done this, so to speak, from the top: attempting to justify certain practices of inequality, arguing either that inequality is natural or that natural equality is compatible with actual inequality. The development of social life in the twentieth century has made it much more difficult, though not impossible, to take this stand; and it has also made it easier to conceptualize social questions from the point of view of those least favoured by the international and national division of labour and goods. The study of social philosophy is essential not only in order to see things in a wider perspective, but also in order to make up one's mind in an informed way about what is to be done.

# Bibliography

## Chapter 2    Feudalism and the social philosophy of Aquinas

Perry Anderson: *Passages from Antiquity to Feudalism* (London: New Left Books, 1974) gives a clear and concise account of both West and Eastern European history from about 1200 B.C. to the rise of absolutism after 1500 A.D., with special reference to the forms of state power. Marc Bloch: *Feudal Society* (London: Routledge & Kegan Paul, 1961) and Georges Duby: *Rural Life and Economy in the Medieval West* (London: Edward Arnold, 1968) are standard works on Western European feudalism. M.M. Postan: *The Medieval Economy and Society* (London: Weidenfeld, 1972; Harmondsworth: Penguin, 1975) is an economic history of Britain in the Middle Ages.

The main work of Thomas Aquinas (1225-74) is the *Summa Theologica* (Sixty vols 1265-73; London: Eyre & Spottiswoode, 1964-76). Of special interest from the point of view of social philosophy are vols 28, 37 and 38. Useful selections are found in Dino Bigongiari (ed.): *The Political Ideas of St Thomas Aquinas*

(London: Hafner, 1953) and A.P. D'Entrèves (ed): *Aquinas, Selected Political Writings* (London: Dent, 1959). The ethics and politics of Aristotle, and St Paul's *Epistles* are highly relevant for understanding Aquinas. Probably the most influential work of medieval social philosophy prior to the work of Aquinas is Augustine: *City of God* (413-26; Harmondsworth: Penguin, 1972). Walter Ullman: *Medieval Political Thought* (Harmondsworth: Penguin, 1965) gives an account of the development leading up to Aquinas's political thought.

## Chapter 3   The crisis of feudalism and the social philosophy of Hobbes

Perry Anderson: *Lineages of the Absolutist State* (London: New Left Books, 1974) is a survey of the development of the state in European countries prior to their bourgeois revolutions. Maurice Dobb: *Studies in the Development of Capitalism* (London: Routledge & Kegan Paul, 1946) contains an account of the transition from feudalism to capitalism. The debate caused by this account is collected in Rodney Hilton (ed.): *The Transition from Feudalism to Capitalism* (London: New Left Books, 1976). Rodney Hilton: *Bond Men Made Free: Medieval Peasant Movements and the English Rising in 1381* (London: Methuen, 1973) gives an account of the medieval peasant movements which blocked the intensification of feudal repression in the West in the wake of the general crisis of the fourteenth century. Lawrence Stone: *The Crisis of the Aristocracy 1558-1641* (Oxford: Oxford University Press, 1967) describes some of the long-term effects which this had for the English ruling class. Christopher Hill: *Reformation to Industrial Revolution* (London: Weidenfeld, 1967; Harmondsworth: Penguin, 1969) is a lucid economic history of Britain 1530-1780. The same author's *The World Turned Upside Down* (London: M.T. Smith, 1972; Harmondsworth: Penguin, 1975) and *The Intellectual Origins of the English Revolution* (Oxford: Oxford University Press, 1965) are excellent histories of ideas of seventeenth-century England.

The central work by Thomas Hobbes (1580-1679) is *Leviathan* (1651; Harmondsworth: Penguin 1968). C.B. Macpherson: *The Political Theory of Possessive Individualism* (Oxford: Oxford University Press, 1962) has a good chapter on Hobbes. Keith Brown (ed.): *Hobbes Studies* (Oxford: Blackwell, 1965) contains many fine articles among which Keith Thomas's 'The social origins of Hobbes's political thought' is of particular interest.

The works of Gerrard Winstanley (*c*.1609-*c*.60) are amongst the earliest available articulations of a systematic radical demand for real equality. See his *The Law of Freedom and Other Writings* (1648-51; Harmondsworth: Penguin, 1973).

Classic discussions of the Reformation are Max Weber: *The Protestant Ethic and the Spirit of Capitalism* (1904-5; London: Allen & Unwin, 1930) and R.H. Tawney: *Religion and the Rise of Capitalism* (London: Murray, 1922; Harmondsworth: Penguin, 1938). An introduction to the ensuing debate is provided by M.J. Kitch (ed.): *Capitalism and the Reformation* (London: Longmans, 1967).

Amongst several works giving clear accounts of the Scientific Revolution, the following may be recommended: J.D. Bernal: *Science in History vol. 2* (London: Watts, 1954; Harmondsworth: Penguin, 1969); E.J. Dijksterhuis: *The Mechanisation of the World Picture* (Oxford: Oxford University Press, 1961); Jonathan Nef: *The Conquest of the Material World* (London: University of Chicago Press, 1964); A. Koyré: *From the Closed World to the Infinite Universe* (London: Johns Hopkins University Press, 1974); and Thomas S. Kuhn: *The Copernican Revolution* (Cambridge, Mass.: Harvard University Press, 1970).

## Chapter 4   Early capitalism: its proponents and opponents

The economic history of England from 1689 to 1780 is covered in Christopher Hill: *Reformation to Industrial Revolution* (London: Weidenfeld, 1967; Harmondsworth: Penguin, 1969). J.H. Plumb: *The Growth of Political Stability in England 1675-1725* (London: Macmillan, 1967; Harmondsworth: Penguin, 1969) gives an account of how the new upper class secured its power after the Glorious Revolution of 1688. E.P. Thompson: *Whigs and Hunters: Making of the Black Act:* (London: Allen Lane, 1975; Harmondsworth: Penguin, 1977) looks at the same process from a different perspective.

The main work of social philosophy by John Locke (1632-1704) is the *Two Treatises of Government* (1690; Cambridge: Cambridge University Press, 1960, with an important introduction by Peter Laslett). The first Treatise is a detailed refutation of the arguments of Robert Filmer: *Patriarcha* (1680; *Patriarcha and other Political Writings of Sir Robert Filmer*, Peter Laslett (ed.), Oxford: Blackwells, 1949), while the second presents Locke's own liberal theory of government. C.B. Macpherson: *The Political Theory of Possessive Individualism* (Oxford: Oxford University Press, 1962) contains a masterly analysis of the theory of property in the second Treatise.

The social philosophy of David Hume (1711-76) is put forward most systematically in *A Treatise of Human Nature Book III* (1738; Oxford, 1941).

The development in France up to the Revolution is outlined in Perry Anderson: *Lineages of the Absolutist State* (London: New Left Books, 1974). Albert Soboul: *The French Revolution 1787-99* (London: New Left Books, 1974) gives an excellent account of its subject matter. Peter Gay: *The Enlightenment* (2 vols, London: Weidenfeld, 1967; London: Wildwood House, 1973) is an integrated history of the French, English, German and Italian enlightenments in the eighteenth century. *The Social Contract* (1762; Harmondsworth: Penguin, 1968) is the central work of social philosophy by Jean-Jacques Rousseau, citizen of Geneva (1712-78). *Émile* (1762; New York: Basic Books, 1979) is his work on education. His views on the education of girls were strongly attacked by Mary Wollstonecraft (1759-97) in her *Vindication of the Rights of Woman* (1792, Harmondsworth: Penguin, 1976).

Edmund Burke (1729-97) reacted to the first phases of the French Revolution in his *Reflections on the Revolution in France* (1790; Harmondsworth: Penguin, 1968). An immediate reply to this attack on the principles of the Revolution was given by Tom Paine (1737-1809) in his *Rights of Man* (1791-2; Harmondsworth: Penguin, 1969). The wider social framework of this debate in England is described in part one of E.P. Thompson: *The Making of the English Working Class* (London: Gollancz, 1963; Harmondsworth: Penguin, 1968).

## Chapter 5 Prussian absolutism and the social philosophy of Kant

Perry Anderson: *Lineages of the Absolutist State* (London: New Left Books, 1974) has a clear chapter on Prussia. W.H. Bruford: *Germany in the Eighteenth Century* (Cambridge: Cambridge University Press, 1935) and H. Holborn: *A History of Modern Germany 1648-1840* (2 vols; London: Eyre & Spottiswoode, 1965) provides much more detail. Peter Gay: *The Enlightenment* (2 vols; London: Weidenfeld, 1966; London: Wildwood House, 1973) covers the German Enlightenment. In the English-speaking world the social philosophy of Immanuel Kant (1724-1804) is known almost exclusively from his short work of moral philosophy *Groundwork of the Metaphysics of Morals* (1785; London: Harper & Row, 1947); this is unfortunate since the social implications of his thought can be understood only on the basis of his *Metaphysics of Morals* (1797-98), Part One of which has been translated by John Ladd as *Metaphysical Elements of Justice* (New York: Bobbs-Merril, 1965), but this edition is seriously incomplete in that sections which show how far Kant was prepared to go in compromising his basic liberal principles are omitted 'as being mainly concerned with technical concepts belonging to eighteenth-century German law'. Ladd continues: 'These concepts are derived from Roman law and do not have any exact counterparts in Anglo-American law. Hence they are of little interest except to the specialist.' (p.67)

## Chapter 6 The Industrial Revolution and its philosophy

The Industrial Revolution in England is described in Phyllis Deane: *The First Industrial Revolution* (Cambridge: Cambridge University Press, 1965); its long-term effects in England are explored in E.J. Hobsbawm: *Industry and Empire: An Economic History of Britain Since 1750* (London: Weidenfeld, 1968; Harmondsworth: Penguin, 1969) and its world-wide effects in the same author's *The Age of Revolution* (London: Weidenfeld, 1962). David S. Landes: *The Unbound Prometheus, Technological Change and Industrial Development in Western Europe from 1750 to the Present*

(Cambridge: Cambridge University Press, 1969) is excellent. The human effects of the Industrial Revolution in England are set out in E.P. Thompson: *The Making of the English Working Class* (London: Gollancz, 1963; Harmondsworth: Penguin, 1968).

The social philosophy of Adam Smith (1723-90), which in many respects belongs to the Enlightenment but which achieved its greatest influence after the rise of industry, is mainly contained in his *The Wealth of Nations* (1776; abridged edition Harmondsworth: Penguin, 1970). R.L. Meek: *Studies in the Labour Theory of Value* (London: Lawrence & Wishart, 1973) has a good chapter on Smith. The frank and grim conclusions of Thomas Malthus (1776-1834) were put forward in his *An Essay on Population* (1798; Harmondsworth: Penguin, 1970). The most famous work of social philosophy by Jeremy Bentham (1748-1832) is his *Principles of Morals and Legislation* (1789; Oxford: Blackwells, 1948). The classic treatment of Bentham and his circle is E. Halévy: *The Growth of Philosophic Radicalism* (London: Faber, 1972). The main works of John Stuart Mill (1806-73) are: *Principles of Political Economy* (1848, Harmondsworth: Penguin, 1970), *On Liberty* (1859), *Utilitarianism* (1863), *Representative Government* (1861) (all three published together, London: Dent, 1972) and *The Subjection of Women* (1869; London: MIT Press, 1971).

C.B. Macpherson: *The Life and Times of Liberal Democracy* (Oxford: Oxford University Press, 1977) discusses the views on democracy of both Bentham and J.S. Mill. Raymond Williams: *Culture and Society 1780-1950* (London: Chatto & Windus, 1958; Harmondsworth: Penguin, 1961) gives an excellent account of conceptual changes following the Industrial Revolution.

## Chapter 7   The modernization of Germany and the social philosophy of Hegel

For Germany in the first half of the nineteenth century see E.J. Hobsbawm: *The Age of Revolution* (London: Weidenfeld, 1962); H. Holborn: *A History of Modern Germany 1648-1840* (London: Eyre & Spottiswoode, 1965) and Theodore S. Hamerow: *Restor-*

*ation, Revolution, Reaction: Economics and Politics in Germany 1815-71* (Princeton, N.J.: Princeton University Press, 1966).

My account of G.W.F. Hegel (1770-1831) is based mainly on his *Philosophy of Right* (1821; Oxford: Oxford Univrsity Press, 1952). Shlomo Avineri: *Hegel's Theory of the Modern State* (Cambridge: Cambridge University Press, 1972), Z.A. Pelczynski (ed.): *Hegel's Political Philosophy* (Cambridge: Cambridge University Press, 1971) and Charles Taylor: *Hegel and Modern Society* (Cambridge: Cambridge University Press, 1978) provide useful, modern interpretations of Hegel's social philosophy.

## Chapter 8    The rise of the working class and socialism

European history from 1848-71 is covered by E.J. Hobsbawm: *The Age of Capital* (London: Weidenfeld, 1975); the German development by Theodore S. Hamerow: *Restoration, Revolution, Reaction* (Princeton, N.J.: Princeton University Press, 1966). The history of the carly organizations within the English working class is described in E.P. Thompson: *The Making of the English Working Class* (London: Gollancz, 1963; Harmondsworth: Penguin, 1968). Many themes in the history of labour are brought together in E.J. Hobsbawm: *Labouring Men* (London: Weidenfeld, 1964) and in Asa Briggs and John Saville (eds.): *Essays in Labour History* (London: Macmillan, 1960; revised edition 1967). Wolfgang Abendroth: *Short History of the European Working Class* (London: New Left Books, 1976) sets the working-class movement in a European context.

*The Critique of Hegel's 'Philosophy of Right'* (1843, but not published till 1927, Cambridge: Cambridge University Press, 1970) by the young Karl Marx (1818-83) is an excellent point of departure for understanding both Marx's debt to Hegel and his criticism of him. *The German Ideology* (1845-6 but not published till 1932; London: Lawrence & Wishart, 1964) by Marx and Friedrich Engels (1820-95) contains an early formulation of the materialist view of history. *The Communist Manifesto* (1847-8, in D. Fernbach (ed): *The Revolutions of 1848* (Harmondsworth: Penguin, 1973) by Marx and Engels is their most immediately influential summing up of the situation and task of the labour movement. See also Marx: *Grundrisse* (1857-8, first published 1939; Harmondsworth: Penguin 1973) and *Capital* (3 vols: vol. I was published in 1867; vol. II and III posthumously in 1885 and 1894 respectively; Harmondsworth: Penguin, 1976).

The life and times of Marx are described in F. Mehring: *Karl Marx* (1918; London: Allen & Unwin, 1936). The author was a leading socialist within the pre-war Second International. David McLellan: *Karl Marx: His Life and Thought* (London: Macmillan, 1973) is more up-to-date and (for better and worse) more scholarly. H. Collins and C. Abramsky: *Karl Marx and the British Labour Movement: Years of the First International* (London: Macmillan, 1965) is an account of just that. For the Second International see vol. III of G.D.H. Cole: *A History of Socialist Thought* (London: Macmillan, 1956).

Central works in the theoretical foundation of reformist socialism are to be found in Eduard Bernstein: *Evolutionary Socialism* (1899; New York: Schocken Books, 1963).

## Chapter 9    Social philosophies in the twentieth century

E. Hallett Carr: *The Russian Revolution from Lenin to Stalin 1917-29* (London: Macmillan, 1979) is a good account of the years from 1917 to 1929. The economic build-up after the revolution is described in Maurice Dobb; *Soviet Economic Development since 1917* (revised edition, London: Routledge & Kegan Paul, 1966). Among the many works by Lenin (1870-1924), *What is to be done?* (1902); *Imperialism, The Highest State of Capitalism* (1916); *State and Revolution* (1917) and *'Left wing' Communism – an Infantile Disorder* (1920) are representative of his social philosophy. They are all published in V.I. Lenin: *Selected Works* (3 vols, Moscow: Progress Publishers, 1967).

The non-Leninist political theory of revolutionary socialism within the Second International is represented by Rosa Luxemburg. See her *Selected Political Writings* (ed. Robert Looker, London: Cape, 1972).

The history of the technology and industry of Western Europe up to the early 1960s is described in D.S. Landes: *The Unbound Prometheus* (Cambridge: Cambridge University Press,

1969) which finishes on a note of great confidence in technological and economic development in the future. Harry Braverman: *Labour and Monopoly Capitalism: The Degradation of Work in the Twentieth Century* (New York: Monthly Review Press, 1974) has a different perspective on the same development. M.M. Postan: *An Economic History of Europe 1945-64* (London: Methuen. 1967); Ernest Mandel: *Late Capitalism* (London: Verso Editions, 1975) and the same author's *The Second Slump: A Marxist Account of the 1974-8 Recession* (London: New Left Books 1978) are Marxist histories of the economy in the Western World since the Second World War.

A good history of the social background of Logical Positivism – the theory which gave individualism a new logical basis – has yet to be written. John Passmore: *A Hundred Years of Philosophy* (London: Duckworth, 1957; Harmondsworth: Penguin, 1970) is informative. A selection of representative works is provided by A.J. Ayer (ed.): *Logical Positivism* (London: Allen & Unwin, 1959). Chapter 6 of his *Language, Truth and Logic* (London: Gollancz, 1936) is an example of the cheerful cynicism of this brisk, no-nonsense approach to questions of moral and thereby social philosophy. John Maynard Keynes (1883-1946): *The General Theory of Employment, Interest and Money* (London: Macmillan, 1936) is the main source of the modification to liberal economic theory which dominated the West European economic policies from the Second World War to the crisis of the 1970s. C.B. Macpherson: *The Life and Times of Liberal Democracy* (Oxford: Oxford University Press, 1977) discusses liberal theories of democracy of the same period.

Perry Anderson: *Considerations on Western Marxism* (London: New Left Books, 1976) and the New Left Review anthology: *Western Marxism: A Critical Reader* (London: New Left Books, 1977) are accounts of revolutionary socialist thought in Western Europe after the Russian Revolution. Martin Jay: *The Dialectical Imagination* (London: Heinemann Educational Books, 1972) is an excellent history of the Frankfurt school. Herbert Marcuse belonged to this school. His work *One Dimensional Man* (London: Routledge & Kegan Paul, 1964) was highly influential in the various anti-authoritarian movements of 1968 and after.

# Index